SAY THIS
THIS

NOT
THAT

To Your Teenage Daughter

DISCLAIMER

This book is not intended to replace medical or psychological treatment.

Ilana Kukoff, Ph.D., and Jessica Yuppa Huddy, M.S. of Applied Psychology, do not practice psychology or psychotherapy. They are the founder, CEO, and Director of Curricula of Cognition Builders, an educational consulting company that provides the *Say This, Not That* program to families across the globe.

The strategies discussed in this book may not be suitable for every individual, and the relationship advice may not be suitable for every family.

If you or a family member have any medical or psychological conditions or limitations you should discuss them, and the advice and strategies suggested in this book, with your own medical and mental health professionals.

In some cases, a family dynamic may require family counseling with a licensed psychologist, psychotherapist, counselor, or other mental health professional.

The names, characters, businesses, places, events, and incidents in this book are either the products of the authors' imagination or are used in a fictitious manner. Any resemblance to actual persons, living or dead, or actual events, is purely coincidental.

This book is not a substitute for mental health therapy.

The authors and publishers specifically disclaim all responsibility for any liability, loss, or risk, personal or otherwise, which is incurred as a consequence, directly or indirectly, of the use and application of any of the contents of this book.

SAY THIS

NOT THAT

To Your Teenage Daughter

The Pocket Guide to Everyday Conversations

Ilana Kukoff and Jessica Yuppa Huddy

Andrews McMeel
PUBLISHING®

CONTENTS

Foreword..vi

Introduction ix

How to Use This Book xii

When She's "So Stressed Out" xiv

When She Doesn't Want You on Her Social Media 4

When She Says She Has No Time for Chores 8

When Her College Apps Still Aren't Done.............................. 12

When There's "Nothing to Talk About".................................. 16

When You Don't Like Her Boyfriend 20

When You Don't Like That Outfit 24

When You Catch Her in a Lie 28

When She Wants to Know Why She Can't "Look Like That".............. 32

When Her Best Friend Turns on Her....................................... 36

When She Wants to Travel Abroad... 40

When She's "Not Going to That" 44

When She Gives You Parenting Advice................................... 48

When She's in a Mood... 52

When You Were Right (Again) 56

When You "Wouldn't Understand".. 60

When She Hates the Way Her Hair Came Out 64

When She Wants to Find a Boyfriend 68

When She Has "Nothing to Wear" 72

When She Raises Her Voice at You.. 76

When She's Embarrassed at School 80

When He Says No to Prom... 84

When You're Moving Out of Town... 88

When She Has "No One to Hang Out With" 92

When She's a Liiiiiittle Ungrateful 96

When She Doesn't Make the Play, the Team, or the Cut 100

When "No One Likes Her" 104

When She Says "But Mom/Dad Said I Could" 108

When Her Room Looks Post-Apocalyptic 112

When She "Hates You So Much".. 116
When He Likes Someone Else 120
When She Has Her First Heartbreak 124
When "*Her* Parents Let *Her* Do It!" 128
When They're Jealous of Her 132
When She's Jealous of Them.. 136
When She Gets into a Fender Bender 140
When She Thought She'd "Have It Figured Out by Now" 144
When You Think She Has an Eating Disorder 148
When You're Getting a Divorce 152
When She Says She Likes Girls 156
When She Thinks She's a He.. 160
When Her Phone Is an Appendage 164
When You Catch Her Sexting 168
When She Drinks Too Much 172
When She's a Bully's Target.. 176
When She's the Bully... 180
When You Want Her to Think Bigger 184
When She Wants to Lose (a Healthy Amount of) Weight 188
When She's Worried About a Big Change 192
When Everything Makes Her Anxious.................................. 196
When the Sadness Isn't Lifting 200
When You Think She's Hurting Herself................................ 204
When Your Family Loses Someone You Love 208
When She Says the Teacher Hates Her............................... 212
When She Steals from You 216
When She Needs to Pick a University 220
When She Wants to Transfer to Another High School.......................... 224
When You Think She Might Be Doing Drugs 228
When You're Very Sick... 232
When You Were Wrong 236

Foreword

||||||||||||||||||||||||||||||||||||||||||||

so much depends
upon

a red wheel
barrow

glazed with rain
water

beside the white
chickens

So wrote the American poet and physician William Carlos Williams decades ago. Kukoff and Huddy, experienced healers in their own right, understand how much depends upon the details: the red (not green) wheel barrow, glazed (not covered) with rain, beside (not on top of) the white (not bantam) chickens.

Unlike so many who offer help to parents, Kukoff and Huddy live in the details, in the weeds, not in the theory. They know what daughters say, and they know how parents writhe in their efforts to respond. They know how hard it is to know what to say. But most of all, they know about that red wheel barrow called reality.

This wise and immensely practical, useful, sanity-saving volume is brilliant in its brevity, scope, and savvy. These two women know what they are talking about (I won't tell you how and why I know this because they have not given me enough space to do so, but, believe me, and you really ought to believe me, because I know) and they can save you sleepless nights, endless fights, and, most of all, help you be the kind of parent you want to be.

No one does the most important job in the world—raising a child—without help. These two women, Ilana Kukoff and Jessica Huddy, give you detailed scripts on what to say, and what not to say, as you "interact" (a euphemism if ever there were one!) with your daughter. But even better, they show you how to use your most powerful tool, the most powerful force in the world—love—constructively, succinctly, and successfully.

Rejoice! The book you hold in your hands will deliver you to a new way of being with your daughter.

Edward (Ned) Hallowell, M.D.

Introduction

Words can make for fickle friends. They are both the chutes and the ladders of our daily lives. We go up and down, from conversation to conflict, often without really knowing why. From the daily common occurrences to the big ticket items, at every turn, the things we say—or don't— shape our lives. Words are never just words. For us at Cognition Builders, this truth is a cornerstone.

Cognition Builders is an educational company devoted to building healthy individuals and families. Ilana Kukoff is the founder and CEO. Jessica Yuppa Huddy is the director of curricula. When we set out to write this book, we thought about the stories we've collected, the conflicts we've dissolved, and the dysfunction we've rewritten. Again and again, our clients ask us so many of the same questions: "What do I say when _____ happens? What do I say when she _____? What do I say every time _____?" So we pulled together the conversational hang-ups we've encountered most often and tackled them, one by one. While no real individuals have been portrayed or named in this book, the anecdotes included are based on the real and composite experiences of our lives, and the lives of those we have helped. Our goal in writing a book has always been clear: bring our method to the masses.

Since our goal is to teach, we knew that *Say This, Not That* needed to be compatible with your real life. Learning is not a passive activity. It may begin with a book, but it never ends there. And every day, we compete against a flurry of distractions, at an unforgiving pace. Chances are that you don't have the time to translate the latest research on adolescent development into workable advice every time you don't know what to say to your teenage daughter. In those moments, you wish someone would just script you (or maybe even censor you). *Say This, Not That* is here to do that.

Cognition Builders has helped A-list entertainers, Fortune 500 CEOs, politicians, and everyday families alike take on the complexities and conflicts of the human condition. The great equalizer in life is having a problem in your family. From more than two decades of experience, here's what we know: It's not theory that saves the day. It's humor, compassion, and no-nonsense instruction.

Introduction

Say This, Not That To Your Teenage Daughter is a pocket guide for on-the-go help. Whether you're in the office, at dinner, or watching a movie with the family, we outline over sixty common occurrences—the moments, interactions, and experiences that make or break our days—and show you how to talk through them.

Ilana Kukoff
Founder and CEO
Cognition Builders

Jessica Yuppa Huddy
Director of Curricula
Senior Assistant Clinical Director
Cognition Builders

How to Use This Book

||||||||||||||||||||||||||||||||||||||||||||||||||||||||||||||||||||||||||||||||||||||||||||||||||

As with any set of instructions, read carefully and follow directly for best results. The same is true for this book. In *Say This, Not That To Your Teenage Daughter*, we cover everything from pettiness to crises. We're not all that interested in why you're saying what you're saying, though we do offer a bit of insight on that. *Why* aren't we interested, you ask? Because we're focused on changing what you're doing, whatever your reasons. Knowing how to respond in the moment is key, and knowing what to say is hard. Luckily, we've taken care of that part. But to make the most of the advice and nail the execution, there are some important things to keep in mind.

Let's lay out the ground rules.

1. Don't be sarcastic. Words go a long way, but tone always comes along for the journey.

2. Don't let emotion do the talking. What you *want* to say and what you *should* say aren't always the same thing.

3. Remember who's in charge. As the parent, it's your job to set her paths, no matter how much pushback you get.

4. A good response is a great start, but actions are always required.

5. It takes years to become the people we are. Remember that your daughter is learning, and that learning takes time and practice. Don't be discouraged if she repeats mistakes.

6. Parent the child you have. Above all else, serve her best interests.

7. Don't assume your daughter is right and don't assume that she's wrong. Talking comes after listening.

8. Don't assume you have to go it alone. At Cognition Builders, we are huge advocates of collaboration and teamwork. Whether the problem is large or small, we love working with clinicians, who consider us to be their eyes and ears into clients' daily lives. We suggest you do the same.

9. Know when you're overmatched. Crises demand crisis interventions. Having a doctor, psychiatrist, psychologist or other suitable professional on board is key when you're concerned for your daughter's safety or wellbeing—or anyone's, for that matter.

10. Preparation is the antidote to *bad conversation*. This book is best used proactively, not in hindsight.

When She's "So Stressed Out"

||||||||||||||||||||||||||||||||||||||||||||||||||||||||||||||||||||||||||||||||||||

It can be puzzling to figure out what to do when your daughter is clearly stressed out, signaling for help, and fully ready to resist any help you might offer.

It's 4:30 p.m. on Wednesday when she announces her arrival from school with a heavy sigh and the thud of her overladen backpack. (It's almost as if she doesn't know that her precious laptop is inside.) She then feels the need to take every single thing out of her backpack and strew them across the dining room table in the most disorganized way imaginable.

Her movements are so obviously overblown that it takes all of your concentration to pretend you don't notice. You're starting to feel as if you're watching one of those infomercials where bad actors pretend to be ridiculously bad at everyday tasks in order to sell you a product you don't need. You are equal parts annoyed and genuinely fascinated. And you're looking almost as awkward as she is, staring at the unfolding scene, not making any clear choices.

Meanwhile, she's begun to glare. *How could she make this any easier for you? What is your actual problem? These are distress calls. Do you have better things to do than to answer them?*

At long last, she comes out with it: "I'm soooo stressed out."

Now you have to do something. Keep in mind:

1. Knowing that something is stressing her out is not the same as knowing what is stressing her out.

2. If she does know what is stressing her out, she isn't likely to explain it well in this particular moment. Just look at what she did to that backpack.

3. You can and should be a part of the investigation regarding what is stressing her out.

SAY THIS

"I hear you. I'm sorry you're stressed. When I'm overwhelmed, I divide up all of the parts of my life to figure out what's stressing me. My life consists of caring for dad, caring for you and your brother, going to work so I can pay for our house, taking care of the pets. Let's divide up your life in the same way. Friends, school . . ."

—

If I ask, she'll tell me what's bothering her, you think naively. Wrong.

Give examples; now it's a multiple choice question.

NOT THAT

"Why are you stressed out? Don't worry about it. It'll be fine!"

———

While you may make light with the best intentions, your daughter thinks you're not taking her seriously. Be sure you know what's wrong before you tell her what's worth worrying about.

When She Doesn't Want You on Her Social Media

Like most people these days, you're probably using social media to stay in touch with friends and family members. It's only natural to want to share some of that joyful connection with your daughter. So what do you do when she locks you out?

There you are on a Wednesday evening, scrolling through a sea of posts from your sister Julie's 30th high school reunion. You double check to make sure that you liked all of the photos. Up next, a clip of two small children auditioning for a big-time singing competition with the caption: "This little girl and boy audition for *X-Factor*." Your friend Phyllis has already commented, "AMAZING!!! The judges' reaction . . . YOU WON'T BELIEVE IT!"

Your daughter *must* see this, so you try posting it to her wall. You bring the cursor to the search bar, type in her first and middle name. Oh, how nice that she uses both! You always told her Rachel Lynn was a beautiful name! But when you click on her profile, you can't see a thing on her page.

Here's why you're being kept out: While you think you're simply sharing a video of children with angelic voices, she thinks that you're attempting to enter the territory of her "tribe." This is the sacred cyberspace where she gets to present her life in a highlight reel of its finest moments. One "like" from Mom or Dad on a well-filtered photo of the California sunset can shatter the carefully crafted illusion that the spring break spent in Los Angeles was not, in fact, part of a family vacation.

The Internet is a social sphere, for better or for worse. And teenagers do not often enjoy including their parents in their social circles. Fortunately, there is a way in. It's just not on most maps. Remember:

1. If the ground is guarded, the territory is vulnerable. Tread lightly.

2. Level the playing field; be as transparent as you'd like her to be.

3. Make your intentions clear; you come in peace, to connect and share. Not to sabotage her online presence.

SAY THIS

"Listen, Facebook/Twitter/Snapchat/Instagram is an opportunity for us to share things we don't get to talk about on a regular basis. We're both so busy that we might get to see something we don't actually know about each other. Feel free to look at my page."

—

Of course she doesn't care about your Facebook posts. She wishes you weren't even on Facebook. The point is to show her that you're willing to be as open as you'd like her to be.

NOT THAT

"If you're on social media, then you don't have privacy anyway."

—

You're right, sort of. Sharing her information publicly is not the same as sharing it directly with you; that's what secret accounts are for.

When She Says She Has No Time for Chores

||||||||||||||||||||||||||||||||||||||||||||||||||||||||||||||||||||||||||||||||||||||||||

As a parent, hearing your teenage daughter say that she's "too busy" to do something you've asked is probably like listening to your supervisor complaining about what to do with a bonus check. But if you can make it past her punishing lack of self-awareness, you will get what you're looking for.

She's running 15 minutes late to the party that started an hour ago. For her, that's about five minutes early. At long last, she's found an outfit that works, part of the elusive 2 percent of clothes in her closet that she actually likes. You knock on the bedroom door, which is slightly ajar, standing cautiously in the threshold. When she invites you to come in, you swing the door open. You're about to venture a compliment, when you see it: the other 98 percent.

Nearly every single piece of clothing she owns—a mishmash of sweaters, dresses, t-shirts, jeans—covers every surface of the room. If you didn't know any better, you might guess that there was no floor at all. Anything that isn't clothing is entirely invisible.

There's no trace of a compliment anywhere. It's long since floated away. In its place: "You *have* to clean this up tomorrow."

You're met with an eye roll, a grunt, a sigh, possibly all three. Then she replies, "You know I don't have time for that! Can you just do it?"

Keep in mind:

1. "No" is not a word she needs help learning.

2. We are all as busy as we feel. This includes her.

3. Time is made, but we aren't born knowing how to make it.

SAY THIS

"We all have responsibilities. I have mine, Dad has his, you have yours. We have to make time to make it work. Let's make a schedule."

—

Most teens are pretty bad at getting past the part when they realize *this is hard*, but, here we are. Show her that you've made it work and that she can, too.

NOT THAT

"If I'm not too busy for laundry, you're not too busy for laundry."/"No one is too busy for laundry."/"Too bad, you're doing the laundry."

—

Many parents are happy to say that their lives are harder than their kids' lives. Don't be that parent. Remember, it's not a competition.

When Her College Apps Still Aren't Done

As a parent, you do a lot of hard things. One of them is watching your teenager take on big responsibilities with shockingly little interest and effort. As uncomfortable as it makes you, your teenager must sometimes take very fragile things into her very careless hands. College applications are one of them.

It's November 2nd (or 3rd, or 4th, or 11th) and the deadline is November 15th. Her laptop is open and warm, her fingers are striking the keys with the same vigor they always do. But it's not the Common Application gracing her screen. The click and clack of her typing are the soundtrack to flighty movements between Facebook, Tumblr, Pinterest, and, once in a while, that English paper she's working on. You ask her, almost rhetorically, how those applications are coming along.

She shrugs. "I've got a lot of homework tonight. I'll look at them tomorrow."

"Sweetie, you know they're due next week."

"Yeah, I know."

"So, how much of them do you have done?"

"I said I'd look at them next week!"

Ah, if only you could just do them for her. You can't—but you can still help.

And while you're rolling up your sleeves:

1. She's doing something high-stakes, tedious, and time-consuming. Think about that combination.

2. Remember that no one avoids something they feel comfortable doing. She's worried—and rightfully so.

3. Don't lose sight of the fact that you and your daughter share a common goal: getting her into the best college for her.

SAY THIS

"So, here's what we're going to do. Tonight after dinner we will sit down together, go through all the colleges, and put the due dates into the calendar. We'll set alarms on the phone that go off a week before they're due. And thank you for letting me know that you're overwhelmed. Now I can help you out."

—

She's not lazy, she's lost. Applying to college is notoriously stressful, boring, and tedious. But you can make it better with good planning.

And if you can't, there are tutors who can.

NOT THAT

"What? Why aren't they done yet?!"

—

This isn't a question; it's a complaint with a question mark at the end. It's hard to come up with something constructive to say when you're freaking out a little.

The same applies to personal statements.

When There's "Nothing to Talk About"

||||||||||||||||||||||||||||||||||||||||||||||||||||||||||||||||

Teenagers are not known for their great conversational skills. In fact, most of the time they have no desire at all to even have a conversation. But as a parent, you're probably willing to drudge through the resistance and land even a brief chat. So, how's that done?

It's a Tuesday, probably. *Isn't it always a Tuesday?* You are filled with equal parts dread and excitement as you bring your Volvo around and into succession at the tail-end of a long line of buses. You drive a few inches, then brake. You drive another few inches, then brake again. It's like you're driving an animated car in a stop-motion movie. When you finally creep up to the front door of the school, you see her sitting on a bench, typing faster than an army code breaker. You allow 15 long seconds to pass before honking the horn.

It's time for the long-awaited lull period between 2:40 p.m. and 3 p.m. in which there is *almost* nothing better to occupy your daughter's time besides you (the phone is a given). Not too long from now, she will be stuck in transit on the car ride between school and home. The second the car door shuts, you head right in.

"So, what's new? What's going on with you?"

"Nothing."

"How's school?"

"Fine."

"What did you do today?"

"I went to school."

In the awkward silence that ensues, remember:

1. She's not lying. There's nothing "going on" with her. It's unclear what that phrase even means.

2. She saw you this morning.

3. No one wants to recap six hours of work the second they step away from it.

SAY THIS

"Let me tell you about something I heard on the radio this morning/read in the Times/Post/ Seventeen/Teen Vogue... *"*

—

The secret to finding something to talk about is having something to say. Reading goes a long way for making good conversation.

NOT THAT

"How was school?"

—

Though you really want to know the answer, this question will never show it. The more detailed the question, the more interesting the answer.

When You Don't Like
Her Boyfriend

|||||||||||||||||||||||||||||||||||||||||||||||||||||||||

The worst pain does not belong to us. It's the pain our children feel. More contagious than a stomach bug. When your teenage daughter's had her heart mishandled, standing idly by is not an option.

She hastily wipes a tear that she will soon deny having shed. You could venture a guess as to what is wrong, but you try to be fair. You stop a few steps short of outright blaming him when you ask, "Are you OK? Is it Jason?"

"Oh, it's nothing," she says with a dismissive wave of her hand. "He was tagged in a photo with his ex-girlfriend this weekend. It was the night he 'couldn't hang out' because he 'already had plans with his friends.' When I confronted him about it, he told me he didn't mention that she would be there because he didn't want me to 'get upset for no reason.' I know I'm being crazy. But it *really* bothers me."

She's not being crazy. But you're about to be.

On the way from 0 to 60, make a pit stop.

Remember:

1. What you tell her to do with her boyfriend has almost nothing to do with what she actually does.

2. This is even more true for parents of teenage daughters.

3. Self-respect takes more than really sound advice. It takes choice.

SAY THIS

"I love you. I know you're not gonna be happy when I say this, but our relationship is based on honesty: I just don't think he's a good match."

—

Give a few examples to support your thesis, but don't repeat them more than once. This is personal, so don't be surprised if an argument ensues. Step away.

NOT THAT

"Break up with him."

—

Forbidden romance. What a turn-on.

When You Don't Like That Outfit

||||||||||||||||||||||||||||||||||||||||||||||||||||||||||||||||||||||

Like most parents, you probably hope that your teenage daughter becomes a sexual being gracefully, eventually; around 25 (or older). At the very least, you may hope that her sexuality is something that happens while you're not looking. None of this is possible. So what do you do when she wants to look sexy?

She descends the stairs with a Cheshire Cat smile . . . and almost nothing else.

Her top is a bra trying feebly to pass for a shirt, failing miserably in the process. Her shorts show so much cheek that for a brief moment you wonder if she accidentally put on a pair of doll pants. You're trying to look at her face, but her chest is pushed so far up and out that you can't look at one without looking at both. She clambers down in shoes that do more to prevent walking than enable it. Awkwardly, and with great concentration, she stalks over to the kitchen. She's leaning on the counter now, lunging forward. The shorts ride higher and you think to yourself: *Apparently, it can get worse.*

She brings her phone a few inches away from her face. Her head tilts, the smile grows somehow more mischievous and she snaps a selfie. "I look good, right?"

Before you answer that, remember:

1. Looking good is not a crime.

2. The more you hate it, the hotter she thinks she looks.

3. There is zero chance she'll wear *anything* she doesn't look "cute" in.

SAY THIS

"Sweetheart, you look great! I like the top, but I don't think it matches with the bottom. Let's see what else you've got in your closet."

—

Her boobs are popping out of that top because that is the whole point of that top. You can make her change her outfit, but you can't change her agenda.

So help her look good without making a fool of herself. Need ideas? Spend a couple of hours with her on Pinterest, leafing through the pages of *Teen Vogue*, or at your local mall.

NOT THAT

"You think you're going out like that?
Go change."

—

The problem with this is she'll pack her real outfit in her purse and change when she gets to her friend's house.

When You Catch Her in a Lie

Whether or not you suspected that your teenager was lying, it feels pretty terrible to catch them. What comes next can be even more intimidating. The denial, the bargaining, excuses . . . it's a truly nasty cycle. Nonetheless, you have to decide what to do next—and fast.

Before you begrudgingly gave her the OK to head out the door, she *swore* to you that Danielle's parents would be home. It was against your better judgment, but she wore you down. To her credit, two weeks went by in which she made her case four separate times a day. That is some persistence. Besides, it's *just* going to be a small get together with a couple of the guys and girls from her grade. It's going to be *super* low-key and *totally* fine. Plus, her parents will be home! At least, that's what you were told.

Then you ran into Danielle's parents at your son's soccer game. And they told you how much fun they had on their 20th anniversary trip last week. (They went to Jamaica!) You try to process the information, faking a smile that probably looks more like a grimace. Then the pieces click into place and an unwelcome clarity falls over you. She *lied*.

When you shuffle in back home, she's sitting on the sofa. She looks up from her screen at you and smiles too happily. "How was the game?"

Before you pounce, remember:

1. She buried the truth on purpose. Don't expect her to come right out with it.

2. Lying serves more than one function. Her reasons matter.

3. You have the power—she knows this. She will act accordingly.

SAY THIS

"Listen, I know you're not being honest with me. So let's talk about who you're hanging out with/how to pace your drinks/the pot smoking/when you got home last night."

—

You're not getting an invitation to this conversation, so invite yourself. There's no better truth serum than guilt.

NOT THAT

"You can tell me anything!"

—

When she does, you get the truth and she gets grounded. It may not be a trap, but she will see it as one.

When She Wants to Know Why She Can't "Look Like That"

Teenage girls rarely get a break from the fight to feel good enough. What do you do when it looks like she's losing a battle?

Playing on the family room TV is the same overlong commercial. A skinny-mini twenty-something dances happily behind floating sheer sheets. Her hair glistens and streams in a slow-motion breeze. She's selling perfume or lingerie or tampons, maybe. You've seen this ad so many times that it's a miracle you haven't memorized it.

You mute the TV to drown out the commercials, but even the silence feels very loud. You chomp awkwardly on some potato chips, then pass them over to your daughter. She is staring, stony-eyed, at the last few seconds of the commercial. And she declines the chip with a look of disgust that feels more than a little unnecessary. Then, as if a private conversation in her head is escaping through her mouth, she asks, "Why can't I just look like her?"

That's a complicated question. So keep in mind:

1. She's looking for an imaginary shortcut to unattainable beauty. Compliments won't do much.

2. She knows what she looks like; so don't tell her what she looks like.

3. Whether or not she listens to you will depend entirely on how you've been listening to her.

SAY THIS

"Think about how many photos you reject before you pick the selfie that gets posted—it may not seem this way, but everyone else is doing that, too. Remember that things are not always what we think they are. If there's a style that you think is cool and would like to try out, let's talk about how to get you there and have some fun with it."

—

There's nothing wrong with wanting to look good. You don't have to promote unrealistic standards to help her explore her sense of style.

NOT THAT

"That's not true! You're just as beautiful! You're very smart . . ."

———

Remember that it's hard to take a compliment from Mom or Dad, even though you're probably right.

When Her Best Friend Turns on Her

||||||||||||||||||||||||||||||||||||||||||||||||||||||||||||

Betrayal stings so badly that the pain can be blinding. Trying to look anywhere beyond it can feel impossible. But you can't run or hide from sabotage. When her friend throws a sucker punch, how can she make a counter move?

She charges into the foyer as the front door swings and shuts behind her with a violent thud. She is breathing heavily, her face flushed. She scans the room impatiently until your eyes meet. The moment they do, hers widen, and she makes a beeline in your direction. In less than a second, she's reached you. Without pausing to put her backpack down, take her jacket off, and without saying hello, she starts in.

"Get this—are you ready? I'm going to tell you, OK, so . . . Sophia told me that she was 'happy for me' and that I should 'go for him.' And *then* when I said I liked him she told me we weren't 'a good match.' And *now* they're both hanging out tonight. They *never* hang out. Oh, and guess who didn't get invited?"

She lets out a sound somewhere between a shriek and a sob. You don't dare point out that Sophia has a long history of undermining your daughter; or that Sophia's behavior does not surprise you in the least.

The fact remains: This hurts. Like a you-know-what. Keep in mind:

1. It's not a good idea to teach your daughter to ignore betrayal. Remember, you're preparing her for life.

2. She will have to deal with the betrayer, in some way or shape, like it or not.

3. She will want to be ready when she does.

SAY THIS

"This is a really painful thing to go through. When my best friend turned on me, it was so hard to think about facing her again, but I had to because I knew I would see her again. Let's practice what you're going to say when you see her. I'll be you, you'll be her, then we'll switch."

———

There are few skills that practice can't improve. Even (and especially) having awkward encounters.

NOT THAT

"Oh, please. You two do this once a week."

—

Before a relationship ends or gets better, a lot of back and forth goes on. This is an emotional tug-of-war; pull for her team.

When She Wants to Travel Abroad

The teenage years are experimental. As a parent of a teenage daughter, you're up against a lot of changes and trial periods: hair dye, piercings, boyfriends, wardrobes—you name it. But what if the unfamiliar territory is *literally* unfamiliar territory? It's bad enough when she wants to go to a party; nevermind a party in Europe. How do you react when she wants to travel to a foreign country; one that maybe even you have never visited?

She moves slowly into the kitchen, hands shaking nervously at her sides. She's fidgeting and grinning nervously, watching your every movement. You stop and look to her, waiting to hear the thing she so clearly wants to say. She shakes her wrists wildly, as if the nerves will shimmy down her arms and onto the floor. You raise your eyebrows impatiently, preparing for the worst. She braces herself, too, and says, "I want to go abroad." As she says this, her voice is so nervous that the statement sounds more like a question. But the words come flooding in after that; the dam broken. "I've been thinking about it a lot. It's a summer program in London that the school offers. Alison and

Faith are going. And it's London, so everyone speaks English there. I've always said that I want to travel and you know that London has been on my bucket list since I was 10. I think it will be really good for me to gain life experience. Plus, it'll look great on my college applications."

You blink a few times, wondering silently what the drinking age is in the UK and why she thinks "life experience" is only available in Europe.

Before you give a one-word response, consider:

1. She's put a lot of thought into this. You should, too.

2. Her dreams matter. So does the way you respond to them.

3. Fear does not make for a good compass.

SAY THIS

"I bet you'd have a great time. Before we make a decision, let's break up the different parts of planning—safety, expense, timing, keeping up with schoolwork—and take care of each. We can start by looking at the cost of flights and seeing how much money you have available right now."

—

Don't shy away from taking big ideas seriously. Instead, show your daughter the relationship between planning and opportunity.

NOT THAT

"Maybe. We'll think about it."

—

Your daughter knows you well enough
to know that "maybe" is a longer way of
saying "no." Whatever the answer is, make it
a clear one.

When She's "Not Going to That"

||||||||||||||||||||||||||||||||||||||||||||||||||||||||||||||

Teenagers like to exercise free will. That can feel like an understatement when asking for even the smallest thing turns into a full-on battle-of-the-wills. Teenagers know how to dig in their heels—and they aren't afraid to do it. So, what do you do when she tries to negotiate a non-negotiable?

You shove the second half of a banana into your mouth and nearly swallow it whole. *Who has time to chew their food?* You're chasing your 10-year-old out the door, when you realize he still doesn't have his coat on. You announce for the thousandth time that it is *January* and that he's putting on a jacket. Period. He huffs dramatically and frowns at you as he slips into the sleeves. It is an unwilling surrender.

You whirl around, looking for your daughter this time. She's sitting at the dining room table, laughing at a text. She, too, is not wearing a coat—or shoes, or clothes that aren't pajamas. "What are you doing?! We need to go!"

With an infuriating lack of concern and zero eye contact, she scoffs, "Oh, I'm not going to that."

Take a deep breath and keep this in mind:

1. It's fun she's after. Deal in her currency.

2. Cooperation and interest aren't the same thing.
   You only need the first.

SAY THIS

"OK, then I'll see you later."

—

Call her bluff. If she makes good on the threat, then give her the cold shoulder. When she disappoints, she should expect disappointment in return.

NOT THAT

"If you go, I'll get you that new bag."

—

If you take a bribe, she will come back with bigger demands. There are better ways to teach commitment.

When She Gives You Parenting Advice

||||||||||||||||||||||||||||||||||||||||||||||||||||||||||||||||||||||||||||||||||

Your teenage daughter is forming her own opinions and that's a good thing. Most of the time, it's nice to hear what she's got to say about just about anything. But what happens when she's suddenly very opinionated . . . about *your* opinions?

You're breathing a sigh of relief as the chaos of the day slows to a stop. You're at the dinner table, finally eating the meal you just spent an hour creating. Hush falls over the table as everyone starts in. The only sound is the cling-clang of forks hitting plates. Then your daughter clears her throat.

"So, I was *thinking* that I could have a little get together this weekend, since you guys won't be around."

You dare to ask: "What's a 'little get together'?"

"It'll just be me, Luisa, Em, Jenna, their boyfriends, and a few of our boyfriends' friends."

"I really don't want that many people in the house when we're not around."

She does not like this comment. "You know, if you don't give kids enough freedom, they rebel. The more you say 'no' to something, the more I want to do it. You know that, right? And if I'm not given responsibility, how will I ever learn anything? I mean, it's not like we're going to do anything stupid! You need to let me have more independence."

Before you disagree with everything she just said, take a deep breath and keep in mind:

1. This isn't about her strongly held beliefs on parenting. It's about that party she called a little get together. Don't be threatened—or distracted.

2. She's only playing parent. You're the real deal. Act accordingly.

SAY THIS

"We really welcome your opinion: We're going to have a family meeting. Feel free to bring this up during that time. Please come up with some specific examples to support your points. It'll help us address them."

—

You may think that you're making your child your equal, but you're really teaching her to advocate for herself effectively. If we want our young women to become problem solvers and world leaders, we can't silence them at home.

NOT THAT

"Come talk to me when you have kids."

—

She's giving you parenting advice as a daughter, not a mom. This is the wrong way to "take it from where it comes."

She wants to talk about your relationship—encourage her to do just that.

When She's in a Mood

||||||||||||||||||||||||||||||||||||||||||||||||||||||||||||||||||||||||||||||||||||||||||||

Teenagers are not always the kindest of creatures. As a parent, you've probably been your daughter's prey more times than you can count. What do you do when she bites the hand that feeds her?

As you graze innocently past your daughter's bedroom, you notice that the door is cracked. It's rare that you gain free access into her world, and you can feel your excitement growing. Catching sight of her through the entryway, you smile instinctively. She doesn't notice. She's lying face up on her bed, staring at the ceiling. And she's watching the wall with so much concentration that she'd beat it in a blinking contest. Your smile falls. She's upset and you need to know why. There is a furrow between her brows that hints at trouble, but you stride right past this warning sign. As your curiosity closes in for the win, you step into her space while she hovers, unhappily, somewhere between worlds.

"Hey, sweetheart—"

Your words are interrupted by a snarl, "*What*?! What do you *want*?!"

It was a trap. You walked straight into the lion's den.

Before you aim your spear, remember:

1. She's in fight or flight mode. If she was OK, she wouldn't be snapping at you.

2. She's trying to shut you out, but it's better if she doesn't.

3. Between the two of you, you've got the better chance of actually solving the problem.

SAY THIS

"It seems like you're upset/frustrated/ disappointed. I love you, you know. Let's get something to eat, rest a while, and talk after."

—

Know your audience and read the room. If you know that she's drained every time she comes home from practice, that's not the moment for a heart-to-heart. And always come prepared with snacks.

NOT THAT

"Just tell me what's wrong!"

—

Don't be impatient; it takes time to figure out how you feel.

When You Were Right (Again)

||||||||||||||||||||||||||||||||||||||||||||||||||||||||||||

Proving your teenage daughter wrong is delicious, but bittersweet. Unfortunately, there's no relationship between how good your advice is and how likely she is to take it. As a parent, you will have plenty of opportunities to smile, raise your eyebrows and say, "I told you so." But isn't a win/win better than a win/lose?

On Monday, you did your parental duty: "Hey, I just want to remind you to email your teacher about being absent on Friday. I would do it now. If you don't do it now you'll forget, and if you get an unexcused absence then he might not let you take the makeup test."

"*Relax*," she cooed. "I'm not going to forget. I'll do it later."

On Friday, she sulks, crosses her arms, hangs her head, and says, "I forgot to send that email. He's not letting me take the makeup test."

And you try very hard not to smirk.

Before you do a victory dance, remember:

1. What it feels like to be wrong.

2. What it feels like to be reminded that you were wrong.

3. Why you give advice in the first place.

4. Whose side you're on.

SAY THIS

"Sweetheart, I'm sorry for what happened. Take a minute to let it all out, then we'll talk about where to go from here. You can email the teacher/write the next due date in your planner/etc."

She didn't want your advice before, but she may want it now. Resist the urge to shove it down her throat. Help her problem solve so she's not sorry she came to you for advice.

NOT THAT

"I told you so."

—

Don't tease her.

When You "Wouldn't Understand"

||||||||||||||||||||||||||||||||||||||||||||||||||||||||

As the parent of a teenage daughter, one of the most mind-boggling challenges you'll face is trying to understand what's happening in her head. In the best of times, it's a tall order. But when she tells you with confidence that you wouldn't understand, you know you're in for it. So, what do you do when you don't understand what you wouldn't understand?

She sits in the passenger seat and lets out a long sigh. You turn your head to see what's up, but she's not looking in your direction. She's only got one headphone in, so she's not totally distracted. You catch her reflection in the window and watch her wipe her eyes. You turn your head back sharply and she does the same, wondering if you saw. The silence grows as the miles roll on, until the car reaches the driveway and comes to a stop. She moves quickly to get out, but you reach for her shoulder.

"Sweetie, you seem upset. What's wrong?"

She looks confused, then annoyed. Her reply is both impatient and conceited. "*Nothing*! There's no point— *you wouldn't understand*."

Before you address that, keep in mind:

1. There are plenty of times when you shouldn't take her word for it. This is one of them.

2. What she says and what she means are two very different things.

3. If you want her to know that you understand, you have to make her feel understood.

SAY THIS

"You know when I took my midterms/when I fought with my best friend/when my boyfriend broke up with me, I found it really, really hard. (Ignore any eye rolls, sighs, or dismissive comments.) You know, when I was in college (insert anecdote illustrating your point—even if it's made up)."

—

Don't allow her to derail the conversation, even if she takes her anger out on you. Tell your story, even if it falls on deaf ears. The message will get through.

NOT THAT

"Why wouldn't I understand?"

—

If you ask that question, you'll get an answer, but it won't be the answer that you're looking for, and it won't lead to conversation.

When She Hates the Way Her Hair Came Out

||||||||||||||||||||||||||||||||||||||||||||||||||||||||||||||||||||||||||||||||||||

A haircut has the power to be one of the worst or best moments in your teenage daughter's life (so far). When she gets a bad 'do, it can feel like the sky is falling down—right onto her hideous hair. So how do you survive the worst case scenario?

You lean against the heavy glass door of the salon and swing it open. As you step back into the fresh air, you exhale loudly, pushing several hours' worth of hairspray out of your lungs. It's been a long morning, but your daughter was *dying* to get her hair done and you *promised* to take her. As you head through the parking lot, you notice she isn't at your side. You pause, looking around for her. You turn and see that she's a few steps behind. Catching her eye, you smile and ask, "So, how do you like your hair?"

She takes a sharp, panicked breath. Her cheeks begin to quiver as tears spill out of her eyes. Between sobs she manages only four words: "I. Hate. My. Hair."

Well, that's one way to waste $60.

Before you start crying, too, remember:

1. If it wasn't that bad, she wouldn't be this upset.

2. How you think it looks means absolutely nothing.

3. Problems that can be fixed, should be fixed.

SAY THIS

"Let's find some pictures of what you really want and go back to the salon. Make sure you tell her what you don't like about your hair so she can fix it."

———

You never get to redo life. You usually get to redo hair.

NOT THAT

"It's just hair."/"It's not so bad."/"It looks good to me."

—

Remember that her hair is a form of self-expression. Whatever anyone else thinks, it's important that she's happy with it.

When She Wants to Find a Boyfriend

||||||||||||||||||||||||||||||||||||||||||||||||||||||||||||||||||||||||||||

You did your best to turn your teenage daughter into a well-adjusted and well-rounded girl. The fact of the matter is that romance is going to be on her mind, no matter how many other important things are there, too. So, what do you do when what she wants is a boyfriend?

She calls shyly for you to come into her room. When you don't arrive within three seconds, she calls your name again impatiently. The call comes one more time before you finally walk into her room. Once you're there, she stumbles. The thing that couldn't wait is suddenly out of reach. You take the reins and start, "So . . ."

She finds her words and asks very seriously: "What's wrong with me?" You open and close your mouth like a fish, unsure of what the question even means, let alone how to begin answering it. Your daughter helps you out. She rephrases: "Why don't I have a boyfriend? All of my friends have boyfriends. I'm the only one who doesn't. No one even likes me! What's wrong with me?"

While you scramble to answer that, remember:

1. Sure, she'll have a boyfriend someday. But she wants one *now*.

2. She *does* care about her schoolwork, her friends, and her hobbies. She also cares about finding a boyfriend. They aren't mutually exclusive.

3. You have an opportunity to teach her what to do when she realizes she wants something. Don't waste it.

SAY THIS

"Let's talk about where you can go to meet someone who's interesting to you. You love art, so let's see if any museums nearby have an event, lecture, or classes coming up. If you see someone cute there, ask them what they think of the exhibit."

—

Good things come to those who try to get them. This is a skill that will carry her all through life. Teach her about creating intimacy of all kinds through shared experiences.

NOT THAT

"You have your whole life to find someone; what are you worried about?"

—

Remember, hindsight comes with age and experience, neither of which she has yet. Validate her feelings and help her find what she's looking for.

When She Has "Nothing to Wear"

As the parent of a teenage daughter, you probably already know that there's no such thing as getting dressed quickly. Your daughter has a process—and a time-consuming one—but she probably doesn't have a *method*. So, what do you do when you're caught in the wild and never-ending saga that is picking out her clothes?

You follow the sound of scattered sighs and moans up the stairs and into her bedroom. As you reach the top, the shrill screeches and unintelligible complaints are joined by the clang of metal crashing onto hardwood. Each dress, t-shirt, and jacket hits the floor in harmony with a grunt or sigh. You watch uncomfortably as she lifts each hanger off the pole, examines it for less than a second, then throws it on the floor. Your suspicions are confirmed; she's trying to find something to wear.

As soon as the realization sets in, she turns on her heel, glaring at you. Your eyes widen in panic, but it's too late. You're in range. She's about to make this your problem.

"I have *nothing* to wear!"

Stay strong. Arm yourself with knowledge:

1. "They're just clothes" is not a true statement.

2. Sadly, and as you can see, having plenty of clothes does not solve this problem.

3. There's a reason she doesn't like any of the things she threw onto the floor. And the reason will unlock the mystery behind this daily crisis.

SAY THIS

"Here's what we're going to do. First, we're going to check the weather for the week. Second, we're going to have ourselves a little fashion show. I'll take pictures. Third, we're going to go through the pictures, pick our favorites, lay out your outfits for the week, and label them. Then you'll know exactly what you're wearing."

—

This is not about clothes. This is about how she wants to present herself to the world. Help her figure out how she wants to be seen.

NOT THAT

"You have so many clothes."/"Just put something on."/"You're just going to school, it doesn't matter what you wear."

She'll probably say: "I'm so sick of all my clothes."/"I have nothing that looks good."/"But I *want* to look *good!*" Then it's your move—and you're back to square one.

When She Raises Her Voice at You

||||||||||||||||||||||||||||||||||||||||||||||||||||||||||||||||||||||

One of the many things teenagers are figuring out how to do is keep their emotions in check. It's a process with a steep learning curve and there is bound to be occasional unpleasantness. But what do you do when she can't find her chill—or any temperature besides white hot rage?

The fourth time she snuck out of the house, you finally say enough's enough. In one of your more badass moments, you tell her decisively that she had been given more than enough chances, that she was not respecting your rules, and that, as warned, you will be taking her phone away. She launches head first into the most determined pleading you've ever heard in your entire life. Promises to never do it again are followed by shameless begging. You learn that she will do *literally anything* to get her phone back. Except wait a week until you give it back, apparently.

At the bitter end of this incredibly long rant, she tips over the edge. In a last burst of desperation, she screams: "I need the phone!"

Stop. Wait. Breathe. And remember:

1. Someone who is screaming is not someone who is thinking. They are mutually exclusive.

2. Toddlers haven't cornered the market on tantrums. See this tirade for what it is.

3. She may not be acting her age, but you had better act yours.

SAY THIS

"We will discuss it when you're feeling less angry."

—

Say it in a cool, even tone; then don't say another word, or you'll scream it. And unfortunately, you can't use blind rage to begin a constructive conversation.

NOT THAT

"Calm down."

—

The best way to show her that you will not be spoken to that way is to not speak to her at all—until she's done yelling.

When She's Embarrassed at School

||||||||||||||||||||||||||||||||||||||||||||

For teenagers, there are few things worse than embarrassment. Even the most non-conforming among them are spending a whole lot of time shaping their personal identities. It comes with the territory of adolescence. So what do you do when she's knocked down more than a few pegs?

The illness comes on so quickly that it's almost as if it happened on cue. The second she arrives home, she announces that she feels terrible and "definitely can't go to school tomorrow." You insist that she take her temperature. She insists that the thermometer is broken. You offer her some aspirin and she forgets that her head hurts. Something's keeping her down, but it's definitely not a cold.

"Sweetie, I have to ask: Did something happen at school?"

The charade dissipates as quickly as it formed and she cries, "I *can't* go to school. I can't even talk about it. Oh my God, I'm *so* embarrassed . . ."

Now that you know what you're up against, remember:

1. Not to underestimate the power of embarrassment.

2. Peers may not be the best mirrors, but they're the ones teens use. What her classmates think matters.

3. Someday it'll all be in the past. Today is not that day.

SAY THIS

"I'm sorry that you were embarrassed. Unfortunately, we all find ourselves in an awkward situation at some point in our lives, myself included. The good news is that the way you talk about what happened will set the tone for how others talk about it. No matter how you feel, you can always play it cool. Let's practice."

—

Teach her the tricks for riding this out; gossip has a high turnover rate. The confidence she fakes might just turn into something real.

NOT THAT

"It'll blow over in a week."/"I'm sure no one even noticed."/"It's just high school, it doesn't matter."

—

Unfortunately, there's no relationship between how embarrassing you *think* this is and how embarrassed she feels. Tell her what to do, not how to feel.

When He Says No to Prom

For decades, prom has sat prettily on its pedestal. It gets its own issue in every teenage magazine. It's the star of movies and songs. If it weren't a rite of passage, it would have gone extinct. When your daughter's crush says no to prom, it's not just any night she loses. What can you do when her teenage dream is dashed?

You frown outside the locked bathroom as her sobs escape quietly beneath the door. You seat yourself on the floor, your own sadness growing. Carefully, slowly, you call her name. She inhales deeply to silence a cry and you know at once that she is hiding. The moment stretches on. When she doesn't speak, you knock and ask directly: "Can I come in?"

She takes another sharp, deep breath and says, "I'm fine."

You wait again, then hear the lock click open. You accept the invitation. You seat yourself at her side and she buries a flushed, wet face into your shoulder.

"What happened, sweetheart?"

The words come out in short, pained bursts.

"I finally asked him to prom. And he said no."

To be of any help, remember:

1. Tread lightly. It's as personal as it feels.

2. You *can* lose something you never had.

3. She has to mourn Plan A before she's ready for Plan B.

SAY THIS

"I know how much you wanted to go with him. It's so rough, sweetie, and I'm sorry. When you're feeling a little better, think about whether you want to ask someone else or do your own thing; it's still your prom and you should try to have fun no matter what. If you want to talk about it, I'm here."

———

The first step to feeling better is agreeing that it hurts. But do remind her whose party it is.

NOT THAT

"Just go with your friends!"

—

Fun with friends was always the plan; it's a romantic evening that's now off the table. Before creating solutions, remember the problem.

When You're Moving Out of Town

IIIIIIIIIIIIIIIIIIIIIIIIIIIIIIIIIIIIIIIIIIIIIIIIIIII

As parents, it can feel impossible to make tough decisions, reach your personal goals, and keep your kids happy at the same time. Competing needs tend to compete, and life throws a large amount of curveballs. When you have to move out of town, every family member is uprooted. But teenagers' roots run especially deep. For your teenage daughter to be happy in a new place, she will need to be gently moved and carefully replanted. How do you manage that?

You learn the news and want to be closer to your mother or father who's fallen ill. Or you learn that the promotion you've sought for years is yours—but it's 2,000 miles away. Downsizing, upsizing, whatever the cause, the outcome for parents is often the same: You've got to make a big move.

When you tell your teenage daughter, she does not take it well. She drags her feet on the packing. Some of this is procrastination, but most of it is sadness. Her friends have all been told and they want to throw her a goodbye party. She doesn't think there's anything to celebrate. After days of watching her stare, ghostlike, at the empty boxes, you decide that you need to talk to her.

Before you do, remember:

1. Every part of her life is changing. Possibly for worse.

2. The friends she'll make aren't nearly as real as the ones she's leaving.

3. When you ask someone to do something very big and difficult, it's good to give as much help as possible.

SAY THIS

"I want to help make this transition as easy as possible. Let's get in touch with the new school and research the clubs and activities they offer. If none of them looks interesting to you, let's talk about clubs that you could start. Don't forget, your friends will still be your friends: Let's also talk about setting up FaceTime chats with them."

—

You may need to relocate, but she still needs a community. Since you can't pack that up in a box, help her get a new one. Make a commitment to go back home once a month or to up your data plan so she can return home virtually. Contact the administration at her new school and get a buddy to give her a tour.

NOT THAT

"Cheer up! You'll make new friends."/
"In a few years, you'll be going to college."

—

You get to control where she lives, but she should control how she feels. Don't deny the problem she's brought up; help her solve it.

When She Has "No One to Hang Out With"

||||||||||||||||||||||||||||||||||||||||||||||||||||||||||||||||||||||||||||||||

A teenage girl wants a lot of different things. Sitting home on the weekend because none of her plans panned out is not one of them. What do you do when one night of boredom brings her to the conclusion that she's completely alone in this world?

It's a Friday night and, besides you, she's the only other person home. You're organizing in the living room when you notice that your daughter is flipping aggressively through the television channels. There's no chance that she's actually consciously aware of what's on the TV; each channel flickers on for less than a second and is traded up as quickly as it came. If there's a show she's trying to find, she's not doing a very good job looking for it.

The second you start watching, the channel flipping gets more theatrical. You take the bait and ask her what's going on.

Her answer is immediate. "I'm so bored. I just want to go out!"

"So go out."

She whips her head around. She's wild-eyed, glaring at you, as if what you just said was the worst thing she's heard in her entire life. She spits the words: "*I have no one to hang out with.*"

Well, that was a trap.

As you claw your way out, remember:

1. Whether she does or does not have someone to hang out with, she feels lonely.

2. Boredom is powerful. Do not underestimate it.

3. If you start listing her friends, she will tell you why every single one of them does not count. She's given this more thought than you have.

SAY THIS

"I know a lot of girls your age feel that way. Let's think about it: You know that Alex and Nicole are busy with soccer, so it makes sense that they're not around. If you tried and the other girls aren't available either, check the school calendar and see if there's an event going on. You know, as people get older, they get more involved in the things that they're interested in. Maybe it's time that we experiment and explore more of your own interests."

—

Lead a quick fact-checking session. She will see for herself that she does, in fact, have friends.

Even if she doesn't, all good friendships live on shared interests. Help her find people that share hers.

NOT THAT

"What about Sophia, Madison, Julia, Rebecca, etc.?"

—

They're busy. And even if they aren't, your daughter will probably tell you they are. Best not to broad brush this: take it one friend at a time.

When She's a Liiiiittle Ungrateful

||||||||||||||||||||||||||||||||||||||||||||||||||||||||||||||||||||||||||||||||||||

Teenagers have a nasty little habit of forgetting that they are not, in fact, the center of the universe. Sometimes, they can be a little less than understanding . . . and a little less than grateful. So what do you do when she forgets both "please" and "thank you"?

Somewhere between booking meetings with your new hotshot client, cooking dinner every night, taking her prom dress shopping and planning your parents' surprise 50th anniversary party, you forgot that she'd asked you for a ride to the mall on Saturday. The morning arrives and you're shoving your wallet into your jeans. As it fights its way back out of your pocket, you check your watch frantically. You're running late to the lunch plans you made weeks ago with a childhood friend who's back in town for the first time in 20 years. As you scramble for your keys, you finally notice that an angry pair of eyes are tracking your movement. Your daughter stands squarely across the room, tapping her foot impatiently. Her expression is a cross between dark delight and total annoyance.

"What's wrong?"

"Oh, nothing. I guess I'll just *walk* 15 miles to the mall."

"Oh, sweetheart. I'm so sorry. I've been so busy that I completely forgot."

"Well, what am I supposed to do?! This is ridiculous. Why can't you remember anything?! I need an outfit for next weekend! What am I supposed to do?!"

To think, you were just about to say that you'd take her on the way over.

Before you do that, remember:

1. Gratitude is the product of experience, not stern lectures.

2. She has no clue how much you have going on.

3. But you can give her one.

SAY THIS

"Tomorrow, I'm going to need you to help out. Here's what I need you to do: cook dinner/ take Luke to school/get your grandparents birthday presents."

—

It's hard to be grateful for work done behind the scenes. Let her take the lead and see what goes into running the show.

NOT THAT

"Do you have any idea how much I work?
Who do you think is paying for college?"

—

The most likely answer is "no." But an extra
helping of responsibility might change that.

When She Doesn't Make the Play, the Team, or the Cut

Growing up is hard to do. When her hopes and dreams are stopped in their tracks, growing up gets that much harder. Her first encounters with rejection have the power to become some of the most defining moments in her life; for better or worse. So, when it's bad news, how do you see her through?

It's the long-awaited moment: the cast list goes up, the varsity spots are filled, or the response to her application arrives. Maybe she clicks open the email with a frenzied rush, or bolts through the hallway to the cork board posting, or rips the envelope so impatiently that it splits in half. The news is exactly what she feared: she didn't make the play, the team, or the cut.

You ask anxiously what the answer was. She shrugs and bites her lip as tears well in her eyes. Neither of you says anything else. What follows in every case is much the same; a cascade of tears, uncertainty, and self-doubt.

As you wonder what you can do, keep in mind:

1. Sometimes, you can't change the outcome.

2. Sometimes, you shouldn't try.

3. Defeat never has to be the defining part of an experience.

SAY THIS

"Sweetheart, I'm so sorry; I wish the outcome were different. I know it's hard to imagine right now, but there is always something you can do to move forward. In this case, I would email the director/teacher/coach and ask for some very honest feedback. Once you get that, we can talk more specifically about how to focus your rehearsing/studying/practice so you'll see real change. Let's also find out if there's a role for you that might better fit your strengths."

—

She doesn't like the hand she was dealt. Show her how to play it, and she might just walk out with all the cards.

When She Doesn't Make the
Play, the Team, or the Cut

NOT THAT

"What?! I'm calling the school!"

—

Don't do, teach. And don't teach entitlement.

When "No One Likes Her"

||||||||||||||||||||||||||||||||||||||||||||||||||||||||||||||||||||||||||||||||||||||||||||||||||||||||||||||||||||||||||||||

Like most parents, you probably want your daughter to have everything she wants. Some of those things are easy to get a hold of. Some of them can be given to her. Other things . . . not so much. So, what do you do when she picks her friends, but they don't pick her?

The car door barely shuts behind her when she announces: "I don't get it." Your teenage daughter is a big fan of suspenseful openings. She leaves out the key information, waiting for you to pose the follow-up question. She's the self-appointed interview subject, and you've been nominated as interviewer.

"What don't you get?" you ask, sticking to the script.

She crosses her arms tightly against her chest, sighs heavily, and groans. As she speaks, her shoulders begin to shrug forcefully up and down. Her arms stay tight against her chest, moving rigidly with her shoulders. It looks as if she's trying to free herself from her own grasp.

The coy opening grows into a conversational whirlwind and the words come flying out. "No one likes me. No one. No one wants to hang out with me. I'm always hearing about the parties after they happen. I'm always bored on the weekends. I think I'm fun. I'm fun, right? I don't get it. No one likes me."

Before you accuse her of melodrama, promise her she's well-liked, or lecture her on the unimportance of popularity, remember:

1. "Included" and "popular" are sisters, not twins.

2. There's a lot of reasons why she wants to be liked. Most of them are good ones.

3. Something triggered these feelings, and it's not nothing.

SAY THIS

"First, I wanna know what being liked means and looks like to you. Make a list of what you think makes someone likable and what makes you likable. We can use it to figure out what you think is missing/how to improve the areas of your life that you feel are lacking in some way."

—

Kill the urge to slam "popularity." And don't confuse it with the desire to feel visible and connected to others—even if she does.

NOT THAT

"In ten years, it's not going to matter how cool you were in high school."

—

Maybe not, but it matters now.

When She Says "But Mom/ Dad Said I Could!"

||||||||||||||||||||||||||||||||||||||||||||||||||||||||||||||||||||||||||||||||||||

As a parent, you know that when your teenage daughter asks for permission, the only answer she's looking for is yes. When that's not the answer she gets from you, she may start looking in other places. But what do you do when she tries to turn your biggest ally?

She's making her way to the door in a tiptoeing creep that screams *she's up to something*. It's the night of the big party you already said she couldn't attend, and suspicions are high. You put on your best poker face and try your hardest to sound casual. In the friendliest tone you can manage, you ask where she's going. To prove just how laid back you are, you don't even bother to look up from your phone.

Several seconds of silence throw you off your game. You give in to temptation and look up at her curiously. She tosses her hair back over her shoulder with the smallest movement. She sticks her chin up while a giddy half-smile spreads across her face. With confidence that borders on arrogance, she says, "Oh, I'm going to Christina's party."

"Excuse me?"

"I'm going to Christina's party."

"I already told you that you aren't allowed."

"Yes. *You* said no . . . but Mom/Dad said I could."

Before you cry treason, remember:

1. Her power depends entirely on you buying it. This is all smoke and mirrors.

2. She may have struck a deal with your ally, but she doesn't have equal rank.

3. Despite her best efforts, you're not really alone.

SAY THIS

"Let's call Mom/Dad now and clear this up so we can all be on the same page."

———

To divide and conquer, you first have to divide. Nip this in the bud.

And if this becomes a repeat problem, it may be worth seeking professional help to make sure that your parenting is on the same page.

NOT THAT

"Why did you ask Mom/Dad after I said you couldn't?!"

—

To undermine you. But, if you're asking her why, you've probably already lost control of the situation. Take the wheel back, no questions asked.

When Her Room Looks Post-Apocalyptic

Teenagers are mysterious creatures. One of their great mysteries: How do they live happily in total filth or disarray? As a parent, you probably have a very different understanding of what a bedroom should look like. So what do you do when your daughter's bedroom isn't just messy, but post-apocalyptic?

You're prepping for your morning run when you realize that your headphones are nowhere to be found. You rack your brain, tracking their movement back through your mind. You sigh as the memory of their last location returns to you. The scene takes place at the kitchen counter, where your daughter slid the headphones across the granite countertop and into her ears. Unfortunately, she's already left for school. Although she'd hate it if she knew, you march toward her room, fully prepared to find and use her pair.

But the second you step into her room, you're horror-struck. The headphones must be long, long gone, sucked into an abyss where organization goes to die. At least three drawers are open and overflowing, spitting socks, underwear, and several bras over their sides. On the floor, her laptop remains on and open, ready and willing to be stepped on. A half-full coffee mug sits cold and abandoned, staining her new pine desk. Her pillows are as far from the bed as they can possibly be without leaving the room itself. A trail of shoes makes its way across the floor, though no two shoes are the same. In their path lies a series of water bottles, most of them full. Her books are stacked unevenly on the floor. This must have been the only place left for them, given that her desk is drowning under a pile of dirty laundry.

As you prepare to confront her on this crisis, keep in mind:

1. She may seriously think her room is clean. You have very different definitions of acceptable living standards; that much is clear.

2. If you don't know where to begin attacking this mess, then neither does she.

3. She doesn't mind living this way. To make this cleanup happen, she's going to need an enforcer.

SAY THIS

"Let's look at our calendars so we can compare schedules and find a two-hour window that works for both of us. Then let's get on Pinterest and get an idea of what an organized room looks like. If you want, we can have an 'organization party'—invite some friends to help you out, then order a pizza after. Or we'll clean it together, just you and me."

—

Don't assume the words "clean up" mean the same thing to you and her. Don't assume that she's got aptitude for it, either. Get in on the ground floor by organizing this organization project.

NOT THAT

*"Oh, my God. It's a nightmare in here.
When are you going to clean it?"*

—

Describing how bad something is does
nothing to make it better. This applies to
messy rooms. Hold off on making judgments
and give instructions.

When She "Hates You So Much"

As the parent of a teenage daughter, you've probably been warned about the woes of raising a teen. Whether it's a sympathetic word, knowing look, pat on the back, or an understanding sigh from a fellow parent, the message has come in many forms and always loud and clear: These are troubling times. It's true, your teenager is going to put more than a few dents in your armor. But what do you do when she pulls the big guns? When the weapon she chooses is the phrase "I hate you so much," how do you survive the wounds?

With unquestionable authority and a sturdy voice, you repeat your verdict a final time: "My answer is still no. There's nothing else to discuss." Her face falls sullenly as she glares at you. "You just don't get it!" Her voice cracks with shrill desperation. She is in the final moments of a fight that's already been lost—and she knows it. You ignore the ongoing protest, matching her defiance with your own stony resistance. Rather than retreat, you busy yourself within the room. After all, you have no reason to feel sorry.

But your daughter isn't finished yet. She begins circling the floor, then you, her eyes narrowing with deadly focus. "*I wish you would just leave me alone.*" You turn away decisively, thinking the better of addressing that. But you enjoy the irony all the same.

Whatever she's doing, it's not working. She reconfigures. What follows must be more biting, more shocking. Before she delivers the final blow, she musters every ounce of bitterness she can manage. Her face burns scarlet red as she begins trembling with rage. She takes a deep, exasperated breath, then screams, "I hate you so much!"

You whip around instinctively, shock knocking you clean off guard.

Before you say a single word, take a deep breath and remember:

1. Teenagers are notoriously impulsive and intense. It's more chemical than personal.

2. "I hate you" is just an empty term for a feeling she doesn't have the patience to explain when she's angry.

3. She wants your attention in the worst way. Don't let her win it like this.

4. As a parent, your job is to know better, speak better, and do better than her.

SAY THIS

"I know you're angry with me for saying no to the party/telling you your homework has to get done before you get out/taking away the phone. We'll talk when you're feeling better."

—

What she said is rude, but this is not an issue of manners. Give her the language to say what she really means, then give her some time to cool off.

NOT THAT

"DON'T YOU DARE TALK TO ME LIKE THAT!"

—

Unfortunately, she already did. Don't get stuck on her wording—it's a distraction from the real problem.

When He Likes
Someone Else

||||||||||||||||||||||||||||||||||||||||||||||||||||||||||||

Your daughter may be number one in your eyes. Unfortunately, the world does not always agree. And when it comes to the boy she likes, anything but first is last. When he likes someone else, the story she planned gets a sad new twist. How can you help her write a happy ending?

You knew well before she finally told you; there was someone she liked a lot. You watched her watch the phone with impatience and hope. You pretended not to notice that the time spent in front of the bathroom mirror grew longer and longer. You smiled when she smoothed out her new shirt and asked hopefully: "How do I look?"

"Beautiful," you assured her.

Soon enough, she started explaining that *he's* going to be there tonight.

On a warm, muggy night that started much like this, she slips back through the front door early. Her hair still holds its pretty curls, though they are frizzier now. She shrugs her shoes off and they hit the ground with a heavy thud. Before she has a chance to say a word, you ask eagerly if there was any *progress*. Her eyes don't move from the ground. You ask again, hoping that she simply didn't hear you the first time. When she looks up, her eyes are dewy. She tips her chin back and she gazes at the ceiling.

"He likes someone else."

Before you go on about how little he deserves her, remember:

1. It hurts to lose the people we like, whether or not we were right to choose them.

2. Hypothetical future boyfriends don't make good consolation prizes.

3. Even painful truths can set you free.

SAY THIS

"I'm sorry. I know it's always uncomfortable and it always hurts. But someone who wouldn't choose you is not going to be right for you. If you were the first or the last person to experience this, there wouldn't be so many songs, movies, and books about exactly what you're going through right now. Let's find an interview with one of the artists you like, talking about a time when it happened to them."

—

You can't always take away the sting, but it helps to remember you're not the first to be stung.

NOT THAT

"It's his loss."/*"You're a much better catch."*/
"He's probably just intimidated by you!"

———

Whatever the reason, it doesn't change the bottom line. She will hurt no matter what, so help her heal.

When She Has Her First Heartbreak

Heartbreak is the ugliest rite of passage. As the parent of a teenage daughter, you probably miss the uncomplicated problems of childhood, like missing board game pieces. When her heart breaks, all you want to do is mend it; if only it was in your power. At the very least, you hope she heals quickly. Is there a way to hurry up that process?

Whether she ended it or he did, whether she cheated or caught him with someone else, whether their downfall was circumstance or distance—heartache is misery. The fact of the matter is that there are a million ways to break a heart and none of them is painless. Sadly, the time will come when she must face it, blurry-eyed and very lonely.

For the second week in a row, she sets her alarm half an hour early. She uses the extra time in the morning to hold ice packs to her eyes, hoping they won't be so puffy by the time she catches the bus. Bed becomes a place she doesn't want to leave, especially on the weekends. You make half-hearted suggestions: maybe she should call her friends and see what they've been up to. Her answer is always "no." The days begin and end the same sad way, and your worry starts to grow bigger.

When you want to fix her heartbreak, remember:

1. You can't see grief out the door until you've let it in.

2. The power of hearing from someone who's lived it. It's easier to reach the light at the end of the tunnel when you're sure that it exists.

3. The road to healing is not uncharted territory. There are lots of maps out there.

SAY THIS

"Sweetheart, I'm so sorry. Let yourself cry and know that it's OK to be sad. We get through heartbreak by maintaining structure and keeping your schedule going. Mourn, but don't allow him to disrupt everything that you've worked so hard for. Let's look into volunteer opportunities as well, so you can devote time and attention to a meaningful cause."

—

Routine may not cure sadness, but it does give it a backseat. Life will bring its share of pain—now is her chance to build perseverance.

This is also a good time to alert the siblings. Encourage your other children to keep your daughter busy. Her heart may be broken, but she's still loved.

NOT THAT

"This too shall pass."

—

It shall, but it hasn't. And until it does,
the wisdom of that statement won't ring true.
She needs help in the here and now.

When *"Her* Parents Let *Her* Do It!"

|||||||||||||||||||||||||||||||||||||||||||||||||||||||||||||||||

Every parent has different ideas about what their teenage daughter should and should not do. You may know exactly why you say "yes," and why you say "no," and your daughter probably does, too. Sadly, this has nothing to do with whether or not she accepts your answer. When she finds out that her friends' parents let them do that thing you won't, she's bound to blow her top. So, how do you recover after you've been *so unfair and so uncool*?!

The injustice of your final answer seems to prevent her from speaking. It's clear she is trying to call foul on the play, but she's struggling to spit out the words, which catch in her throat and never make it to her mouth. In their place is a series of stammers, sighs, tuts, and groans. After about a minute of this, she throws her head backward in absolute anguish. You can't tell anymore who she's annoyed with—you or herself.

She let her anger get the best of her. She realizes this and regroups. She lifts her head back up again, slowly, (probably for dramatic effect). She glares at you briefly, then stares down at the floor. As she begins to pace, her brow furrows in concentration. The stakes are high and she is racking her brains to find a way to what she wants to hear. Suddenly, her eyes widen. She's found it. She looks back up at you in a giddy rush. Hardly containing herself this time, she shrieks, "but . . . but . . . Sam's parents let *her* do it!"

Whether or not this is a curveball for you, remember:

1. Don't be distracted by new information. She wants to throw you off and change your mind.

2. Rules aren't up for negotiation.

3. You never have to justify a rule—but you should explain why it's there.

SAY THIS

"If you want to talk about why I feel this rule is important, you know that I'm always willing to do that. But you should know, it won't be a negotiation. If you're looking to change the outcome, the conversation won't be worth your time."

———

Don't discourage her from understanding the moral of the story, but don't rewrite the ending.

NOT THAT

"She *is not my problem. You are.*"

—

"Problem" probably isn't the best word.
Your daughter doesn't have to agree with
your call, but she should understand it. Give
your rationale and redirect her back to center.

When They're Jealous of Her

When it comes to jealousy, teenage girls may take the cake. They are the supreme queens of passive aggression and saying everything except what they mean. This is never truer than when what they're feeling is something they'd never admit. When the not-so-subtle signs all point to a jealous friend, how can you help your daughter beat the green monster?

She bites her lip in concentration. She looks up at you a few times before she begins to speak. Even then, she seems unsure that she should be saying what she's saying.

"Can I ask you something?"

"Sure, sweetie."

"I guess it's not a question, really. Just . . . something's up with Kayla. She didn't text me when she heard that I got the lead in the play, and she knows how much I wanted that. Then today, at lunch, she was awkward and weird. I mentioned that rehearsals started this week and she said, 'Oh my God, will you shut up about that already?' And last week, I texted her about Saturday she said she didn't know if anything was going on. And then today, I saw pictures of her with

Kelsey, Noel, Jo, Sophia—everyone. They went out and she didn't tell me. I'm 100 percent sure she's avoiding me and I have no idea why."

You have an idea why. Before you break it to her, remember:

1. Kayla wants your daughter to ignore her attitude.

2. It's tempting for her to ignore it, but she shouldn't.

3. The best way to fight passive aggression? Direct conversation.

SAY THIS

"Sounds to me like Kayla is feeling a little jealous of you. The best thing that you can do is call Kayla on the phone tonight, or talk to her first thing when you see her in school. Tell Kayla you're sorry she didn't get the part, that you don't want it to get in the way of your friendship, and that you want her to be happy for you like you are happy for her."

—

Conflict and confrontation are facts of life and high school is a microcosm of the real world. When it comes to learning to shoot straight, start them young.

NOT THAT

"She's jealous of you, of course. Look at you."

—

Whether or not that's true, jealousy is not something you want your daughter to take pride in.

When She's Jealous of Them

||||||||||||||||||||||||||||||||||||||||||||||||||||||||||||||||||||||||||||

Comparison may be a thief of joy, but it's a thief your daughter is in cahoots with. When she wants what she can't have (or thinks she can't have) things can get uglier than a green monster. So, how can you spare her the misery of jealousy?

She's bypassed the daily check-in with cyberspace for something much more focused. The usually slow scroll-then-double-tap routine has been replaced by something much more aggressive. Her thumb flies hastily up and down the screen, faster than the pictures can load. She's either afraid to look at them, or desperate to see every one in as little time as humanly possible. Maybe she's both.

She stops sharply, then changes direction; rewinding the pictures back to the top of the page. She finally picks an image, clicks on it, and stares at it. You try to steal a look to discover the object of her most recent fascination. You're not surprised to see that she's been glued to one account, clicking on and off pictures of the same person. She checks over her shoulder cautiously; she doesn't want to be noticed. Too nervous to carry on, she sets the phone aside.

After a minute or two, she relaxes, then picks it up again. She didn't notice that you noticed. You back away slowly, hoping to keep it that way. Then she calls for you.

In the most innocent voice you can manage, you ask her what's up.

"Can I ask you something?" Before you can answer, she asks you something: "What do you think of *her*?" She holds the phone an inch from your face. The screen is adorned with a classmate of hers that you recognize, but don't know. Before you can respond, she continues, "Tell me. Honestly. She's not that cute, right? If you think so, tell me though. Everyone thinks that she's gorgeous. I mean, she's pretty, I guess. Her hair always looks good and she's skinny and all that. She's probably going to win the nicest eyes award . . . but I don't see it."

Skeptical? You should be. But remember:

1. You can't take a good, hard look at yourself if you're too busy staring at someone else.

2. Whatever your daughter's got going for her, she can't think of right now. You can change that.

SAY THIS

"I want you to make a list of 10 things that only you have and how they've helped you grow as a person. I'll help you write it. Then I want you to say five of those things aloud, once each morning and once at night. I'll do it with you."

—

It's one thing to like who you are, it's another to say it aloud. Like all good things, self-esteem is made from the ground up.

NOT THAT

"You've got so much going for you!"/"Don't worry about them. Worry about you."

—

It's not worry, it's jealousy, and you can't stop her from noticing other people's success.

When She Gets into a Fender Bender

|||||||||||||||||||||||||||||||||||||||||||||||||||||||||||||||||||||||||||||||

As the parent of a teenager, some of the worst words you can ever hear are: "I got into an accident." When you get this dreaded call, it's hard to know which way is up. Once you exit crisis mode, you're still left with a damaged car. A lot of things need fixing. How can you repair them?

Your brain has left the building and your body is on autopilot. You race to the scene so quickly that you risk causing an accident yourself. Your senses do not return until you see her standing beside the car, scattered, shaky, but otherwise unharmed. Her arms are drawn protectively across her chest as she sways nervously in the cold. She's speaking with a police officer, but her eyes are wide and far away. As you run toward them, she turns around. At the sight of your face, she bursts into tears and starts in, "I'm so sorry, I'm so sorry, I'm so sorry, I didn't mean to, it happened so fast, I'm so sorry . . . the car is not that bad, it's not totaled, I don't think it's totaled, I'm so sorry, I . . ."

Let out the biggest sigh of relief you have ever breathed, then remember:

1. She's OK, and nothing is more important than that. Tell her, she needs to hear it.

2. Teenagers are new drivers. Take pity on the amateur.

3. When her car takes a hit, so does her bank account. Expensive inconveniences make for good life lessons.

SAY THIS

"First of all, I'm glad that you're OK. Are you in a safe place to talk? Make sure you've pulled the car over safely. Let me know where you are so I can meet you. I know this is stressful, but it has happened to all of us at some point. While you're waiting for me, let's review what to do. First, call the police to report the accident. If you're OK and the other person is OK, the next step is to make sure you get pictures of both cars. If the other driver is calm, ask for their vehicle registration and take a picture of it. When the police officer arrives, write down his badge number and ask him when the accident report will be ready. Once you get home, we will figure out how you can save enough money from work/chores/allowance to pay the deductible."

—

When life gives you lemons, teach your daughter how to handle the unexpected.

NOT THAT

"I knew this would happen!/This is why you don't buy a teenager a car."

—

Unfortunately, "undo" is not an option, so you'll need to find another way out.

When She Thought She'd "Have It Figured Out by Now"

Your teenage daughter gives a lot of thought to who she is and who she wants to be. When what she has and what she wants don't overlap, disappointment follows. The teen years come with a lot of questions, one more complicated than the next. When they aren't answered quickly enough, your daughter will itch with impatience. What do you do when she wants her whole life organized before she reaches the ripe old age of 20?

She tosses the latest acceptance letter carelessly onto the counter, barely glancing at it. You stare at the document, then at her, dumbfounded. You've never seen a less enthusiastic reaction. She shrugs and says nothing. You ask, "which school is that from?"

"Pace, I think."

"That's incredible! Congratulations!"

Another shrug.

"What's wrong?"

She sighs and looks up at you. Her shoulders lift and fall heavily beneath an unknown weight. She purses her lips, frowns, and thinks for another moment. Then she starts, her confession almost angry: "I have no clue where I want to go to college and I have no clue what I want to major in. I don't have a prom date, let alone a boyfriend. I don't even know what I'm good at. How am I supposed to pick a college, or a career? I can hardly pick out what I want to wear in the morning. What am I doing? I have no idea. I thought I'd have it figured out by now."

Before you belittle this concern, remember:

1. She's making a lot of big decisions, for the first time, right in a row. That's very hard to do.

2. It is, in fact, possible to organize your life. It's also a good idea.

SAY THIS

"It's normal to think that; it's what most girls your age think. It can be disappointing and overwhelming to feel like you're not where you want to be. Let's talk about how you can figure out how to meet any goal in your life, moving forward. We can make a training schedule to improve your running/rank the colleges you're interested in/talk about strategies for networking at your summer internship."

———

Figure out what needs figuring out. Once you've helped define her goals, make a plan for reaching them.

NOT THAT

"No one has it figured out by now!"

—

Without meaning to, you just asked her to support her argument. When she does, you'll be back to square one.

When You Think She Has an Eating Disorder

‖‖

Sadly and more than any other group, teenage girls are bombarded with the message that thinner is better. It creeps up in places you'd expect and places you wouldn't; from television to dressing rooms to the classroom. The pressure is on; and it can feel inescapable. For your teenage daughter, it can even kick-start a mission to lose weight. But what do you do when that mission takes a very unhealthy turn?

At first, you don't give very much thought to her declaration that she, "needs to lose weight." Skinny talk has been the standard since she reached age 13. But things have started to shift. After spending 4 hours at the gym on a Saturday, she told you offhandedly, "I could have stayed a little longer." You asked her bewilderedly how that could possibly be, but she didn't answer your question. At dinner, she moved her food across the plate meticulously, slowly, repetitively. By the end of the meal, the food remaining was exactly the same, just arranged in a lump on the corner of the plate. You frowned at her and remarked, "you didn't eat anything." But she grinned reassuringly and said, "I'm so full!"

As your worry starts to build, remember:

1. Little good will come from pointing out her size. She's already hyper-focused on that.

2. When approaching big problems, it's easier to take baby steps.

3. True eating disorders aren't just about being skinny. The roots run much deeper. Pull all of them.

4. Eating disorders are extremely serious and require professional support. If you are concerned that your daughter has an eating disorder, seek professional support immediately.

SAY THIS

"I see that you aren't eating at meals."/"I see that you have been exercising for 4 hours a day, every day."/"I hear you getting sick in the bathroom after eating. I love you. It makes me sad and afraid to watch this happen."

"We're going to make a list of some of the things we can do together to make you healthier. It's time for your physical anyway, so we're going to make an appointment."

—

The first time you hear her throwing up and it's not from the flu—take her to the doctor. They're your first line of defense. Don't sit on your suspicions; this is no small thing. Watch her like a hawk, even if that means you're sleeping in her bed. Now is not the time to concern yourself with privacy.

NOT THAT

"You're way too skinny!"/"You need to gain weight."

———

When you tell her that she looks skinny, she thinks: *It's working.* Take the emphasis off her weight—the problem is much deeper.

If you notice something is wrong with the way your daughter looks or acts, it's time seek support from a professional.

When You're Getting a Divorce

||||||||||||||||||||||||||||||||||||||||||||||||||||||||||||||||||||||||||||||

One of the hardest things anyone can go through in life is divorce. As you mourn the past that's gone, the present that's shifting, and the future that will never be, it's hard enough to hold yourself together, let alone your teenage daughter. But neither your feelings nor hers can be left unaddressed. There is much to say, none of it easily said. How do you tell your daughter that her family is about to change?

You look at your partner with longing and sadness. They meet your eyes and smile sympathetically before their face falls, too. You frown together in unhappy recognition. You have not agreed on everything—sometimes it felt like you didn't agree on anything. But you share the heavy dread that hangs over your heads. You both know what must be done, what must come next, and neither of you feels prepared to do it.

The fact that you are getting a divorce may not take your daughter completely by surprise, but until now, it was only a possibility. With the papers signed and the process nearly finalized, you can no longer hold off on telling her. It's official.

You close your eyes, stalling for just one more moment. When it's gone, you open your eyes and start unsteadily toward her bedroom.

To make this painful talk a little less so:

1. Do it together. Your daughter needs to know that *both* of her parents are still her parents.

2. Focus on the reasons why divorce was the best way forward, not the reasons why the marriage didn't work.

3. Encourage her to share her thoughts and feelings. She may not be a part of the marriage, but she's a part of the family.

SAY THIS

"Mom/Dad and I want to talk to you. Just so you know, we want to include you in the conversations that affect our family as much as we possibly can. We've made the decision to get a divorce. We know you're going to be upset and we're here for you. We both love and treasure you. We want to hear whatever you want to say."

—

Leave space for her sadness, grief, and confusion. The marriage was yours, but the family is hers, too.

NOT THAT

*"Your Mom/Dad and I are getting a divorce.
We tried to make it work, but we just can't."*

—

When the news is delivered in passing, your daughter will feel like an afterthought. Give her some ground to stand on while her world is shaken up.

When She Says
She Likes Girls

||||||||||||||||||||||||||||||||||||||||||||||||||||||||||||||||||

As the parent of a teenage daughter, there are plenty of conversations you've prepared for. They usually sprout up around rites of passage and milestones. They end with phrases like "drive safely" or "maybe when you're a little older." But when your teenage daughter says that she likes girls, the conversation that follows may be one you never thought you'd have. How do you respond to one of the most personal, important, and courageous truths she'll ever share with you—with zero preparation?

On an otherwise ordinary day, your daughter asks if she can speak with you, alone. You tell her that you'll be right up after you finish your final work email of the day. A few minutes later, you close your laptop with a satisfied snap and the day's last ounce of stress melts away. You aren't sure what to expect as you meander down the hallway toward her room, but you don't give it all that much thought, either. You raise your arm to knock on the closed door, but she calls to you to come in before your hand can touch the wood.

She's biting her nails, eyes fixed on the floor in front of her. You start to ask if everything is OK, but she begins to speak.

"There's something—I've wanted to tell you for a while, but I didn't know if . . . do you want to sit? No? That's OK . . . I wanted to wait for the right time. And I don't know if this is it, but I need you to know. I can't wait anymore. It's been weighing on me; I'm so tired of worrying about every word I say, worrying that I may slip up . . . I don't know what you'll think but that's worse, somehow, than guessing and it's all just too much. So, I have to say it, I have to get it off my chest . . . I like girls."

No matter what you're thinking now, remember:

1. If you're surprised, that's by design.

2. It's not about you. Does your sexuality have anything to do with your parents? Neither does hers.

3. She's not saying this for shock value. She's definitely not saying it for fun. She's saying it because it's true, because she loves you, and because she thought you ought to know.

4. Your first and most important job is to love her completely and unconditionally. Act accordingly.

SAY THIS

"I know this must be hard to talk about.
Thank you for letting me in. I love and support
you no matter what. I want to help you as you
learn more and more about yourself. Let's talk
about some different ways to do that, like join-
ing a group—whether online or in person—or
simply connecting with others who have shared
this experience."

—

No matter what you're feeling, this moment
will forever be recorded into family history. It
can never be undone. Be the audience member
you'd want, while baring your heart and soul.

NOT THAT

"Was there something we did?"/"How did we miss this?"/"It's a phase."/"What about the crush you used to have on _____?"

———

When you answer her revelation with questions or denial, you reveal your disappointment. Whatever your feelings are, in this moment, hers come first.

Save your questions, but educate yourself. Now is the time to read articles, books, and find your own support group.

When She Thinks She's a He

||||||||||||||||||||||||||||||||||||||||||||||||

When you think about the hopes you have for your daughter's life, there are probably a million and one spectacular things that come to mind. But no matter how vivid your imagination or wild your dreams, the simplest desires still trump them all: safety, health, happiness. When your teenage daughter identifies as transgender, it's easy to feel like these most basic things are threatened. How do you talk to your daughter when she's not sure that's who she is?

Your frame is motionless, except for the slow rise and fall of your chest. You replay the words on an audio loop in your mind, waiting for them to come together in a way that makes sense. A quiet voice inside your head reminds you that it's been too long since you've spoken; you must say something, soon. You rewind, then press fast forward, listening carefully, hurrying to understand.

"I've always felt different from everyone else . . ." she'd said.

"You know that I've never been interested in the same things as other girls my age, since I was little . . ."

"I always felt that something wasn't right. For a very long time, I didn't know what it was . . ."

"Lately I've been questioning my identity . . ."

"I think that I'm transgender."

Keep breathing and remember:

1. How well (s)he manages has a lot to do with how well you do.

2. You can't make a safe haven in the outside world. Make sure (s)he has one at home.

3. (S)he doesn't have to be a daughter to be your child.

SAY THIS

"I support and love you unconditionally. Thank you for sharing your honest feelings and self with me.

I want to help you with this. I'm going to be learning with you, so it would really help to have feedback on what I'm saying and doing— what's helpful to you and what's not.

Please let me know if there are different pronouns or names you'd like to use and how I can help you find community. Let's make an appointment with our primary care physician and a mental health professional, so you can have the support you need."

—

This is a moment that will set the tone for a lifelong conversation. Be collected, be supportive, and know that her needs are best served with the help of a professional.

NOT THAT

"I don't understand . . ."

—

In a moment as monumental as this, the words you say—or don't say—shape the dynamic of your relationship. The memory won't ever leave either of you. Make it a good one.

When Her Phone Is an Appendage

||||||||||||||||||||||||||||||||||||||||||||||||||||||||||||||||||||||||||||

Getting a teenage girl's undivided attention is about as easy as catching a unicorn. Unless you're a cellphone, in which case all you have to do is be yourself. When it comes to the unbreakable bond between girl and phone, how does a measly parent like yourself sever the ties?

Before she picks her own body out of bed, she picks her phone up from the nightstand, where it rests loyally each night, waiting. In the early morning commute, she cradles it between both hands, thumbs bouncing up and down atop the bright bluish light. She lets out a small laugh. You turn eagerly in search of the cause, only to realize it's the screen. Whatever it was, it wasn't meant for your eyes. You drive on, enjoying the morning sun and thinking that it's shame that she won't see it.

When she walks back through the door some hours later, you give a cheerful hello. Her half-hearted "hey" returns five long seconds later, as if you're TV reporters corresponding from opposite coasts. She doesn't look up, but you're unfazed. Eye contact is a dream that died the day she got her first cellphone.

As she makes her way into the foyer, it's memory, not eyesight, guiding her steps. It never occurs to her that she should probably stop texting to look where she's going. And then, finally, it occurs to *you*: This has gotten out of hand. Her phone has become an appendage.

Before you begin a full-blown intervention, remember:

1. Everything in moderation. She doesn't have to get off the grid to take it down a notch.

2. To that end, a sweeping ban is not likely to work. What is it they say about absence and the heart?

3. Choose your moment. If you don't let her finish that text, she's not going to think about anything else.

SAY THIS

"As soon as you're finished, please put the phone down and put it on silent. It'll help us both concentrate. I'm going to do the same."

—

Lead by example. To get undivided attention, give undivided attention.

If you show that it's hard for you to put down the phone, even better. Then she'll know that you understand *and* appreciate her doing the same.

NOT THAT

"You are addicted to that thing!"/"Sure, I'll wait."/"Put that thing down and look at me for a second!"

—

You've given her a place to put her anger, but not her attention. All she can hear is your annoyance.

If you want to invite conversation, be inviting.

When You Catch Her Sexting

||||||||||||||||||||||||||||||||||||||||||||||||||||||

As a parent, there are a lot of things you hope you'll never see. It feels safe to assume that anything to do with your teenage daughter's sex life fits squarely into that category. That includes sexts, which might also be filed under the category of things you hope will never even *exist*. When you catch her sexting, it's 0 for 2. What do you do after you've seen the unseeable?

There's no answer to the first or second knock, so you turn the knob and call her name, letting your voice leak through the cracked door. The walls let out a low hum as the water begins to run. *She must have stepped into the shower.* Confident that you won't find her there, you see yourself into her bedroom without waiting for an invitation.

As you collect the clothes in and around the laundry basket, her phone buzzes with the chirp and drum of an incoming text. The screen was left face up and you check the message instinctively.

GREAT shot. Tx for sending ;)

Your whole body turns rigid, except for your heart, which beats savagely against your rib cage. You hold your hinged breath as you force yourself to slide your thumb down half an inch.

Then, with one eye closed, you see it.

Before you gouge out your eyes and throw her phone into the fireplace, remember:

1. What it was like to have teenage hormones.

2. Assuming you're comfortable with your daughter having a sex life, make sure it's a safe one.

3. Shame is learned. Don't teach it.

SAY THIS

"Now is your time to learn about yourself and to come into your own, especially when it comes to sexuality. Here's the problem with sexting: Once you hit send, someone else takes control. I always want you to be safe and empowered. Let's talk seriously about ways you can flirt or connect without taking unnecessary risks, and let's get you an appointment with a gynecologist. I'll go with you."

—

Growing up can't be stopped, but poor choices can. This is where a cautionary tale is always worth sharing. Google some real-life horror stories about girls, just like her, who hit send.

NOT THAT

"He's going to send them to the whole school!"

—

Insecurity and shame will shut down the conversation before it starts. Make sure your voice of reason sounds reasonable.

When She Drinks Too Much

As the parent of a teenage daughter, you probably expect to tackle drinking, whether you don't mind her knocking back a glass or two or don't want her to have a single sip. Either way, something must be done when she drinks too much. So, what do you do with a drunken teenager?

It's 2:58 a.m. on a Friday night—make that Saturday morning—when the screechy creak of the back door scares you awake. Feeling more annoyed than concerned, you roll over, deciding not to worry about whatever just walked into the house. Then the screen door closes with a clumsy thud. You groan and throw the covers off.

You stumble down the stairs, a little stupefied, somewhere between the states of asleep and awake. All the lights are out except for one, and it belongs to the open refrigerator. Someone is rummaging in there loudly. You squint at the figure digging clumsily through the shelves. If you weren't concerned before, you definitely are now. At the sight of you, your daughter turns sharply, jumps, and lets out a little yell. Then she slaps her knee and starts giggling. "Heeeeeey! Oh my gah, you scared me! Did I wake you up? I'mmm I'm sorry!"

More laughter. She pivots, snaps the refrigerator door shut in a whirl, then staggers over to you. "What's up?"

"Are you drunk?"

"What?! No, no. I'm fi—" her last word is interrupted by a belch. Her face goes ghostly white, then falls. She hurls toward the bathroom like a runner in the final seconds of an Olympic sprint.

When you confront her on this (and when she's not throwing up), remember:

1. Drunk people don't make good listeners. Save this chit-chat for when she's sobered up.

2. Drinking is not the worst thing she could do. Drinking and driving is. If she didn't bring the car back home, that's probably for the best.

3. Drinking may be fun, but puking is not. You can play the vomit card.

SAY THIS

"I'm really glad you were responsible enough to get a ride, and I'm glad you came home. Let's make sure you sleep on your side tonight. I'm going to see you off to bed. I'm going to get a garbage pail to leave by your bed and prop some towels up behind you so you don't roll onto your back. Tomorrow, I want to talk about what we can do to prevent this from happening again."

———

It's important to consider whether there have been addictions in your family. It's also important to consider how frequently she's come home intoxicated, how many drinks she's had, who your daughter is drinking with, and whether she is under the legal drinking age.

If her drinking poses risk to her health and wellbeing or you think that your daughter may have a drinking problem, consult a mental health professional immediately.

NOT THAT

"Don't you ever come home drunk again!"

—

Unfortunately, these instructions leave a lot of room for interpretation. Don't discourage honesty in your attempt to discourage drinking.

When She's a Bully's Target

Conflict and self-doubt are two terrible villains of the teenage years. Alone, they can be fought, but when a bully wields them as a weapon, the fight gets harder. As a parent, there are few things worse than watching your daughter dim with sadness and greet the days with dread. When she's become a bully's target, how do you give her back her power?

The first sign that something is seriously wrong is that her cell has gone untouched for so long it's practically collecting dust. When messages do come in, she nearly jumps at the sound. It's the same high-pitched chirp that has always told her there's a new text, but they trigger a very different reaction, now. For someone who has a sudden and total lack of interest in the device, however, she certainly doesn't want *you* anywhere near it. As soon as you're in the same room as her phone, she scoops it up and shoves it into her pocket so forcefully that you wonder how her pants haven't ripped yet.

Her computer suffers similar treatment. When she's not doing homework, it stays tight-lipped and uncharged, hiding in its sleeve beneath her bed. Using it seems to bring her stress.

Then, it's Monday morning again. She turns her spoon around the cereal bowl, watching it spin. Although her lights were out by 11 the night before, her eyes are red and dressed in dark circles. For a few minutes, the only sound is the clink of the metal spoon against the ceramic. Then, breathlessly and without looking up, she says: "She won't leave me alone . . . I tried to ignore her, I did, but she won't stop . . . it's horrible, it's horrible . . . I can't to go back to school."

Listen carefully to what she's saying and before you speak, remember:

1. The problem is so bad that she doesn't think she can face it. If you're wondering whether it's a big deal, there's your answer.

2. If she's not heard now, she may not speak up again.

3. This cannot continue. If she doesn't call for action, you better do it.

SAY THIS

*"I'm sorry that you've been suffering, and
I'm sorry that I didn't know about it until now.
You don't deserve to be treated the way they
treat you. With our support, we're going to put
a stop to this. First, let's talk about the specifics
of what he/she is doing: when, where, and how.
Then we're going to determine the best way to
deal with every situation."*

———

Kill them with kindne . . . STRATEGY,
STAMINA, AND TEAMWORK. Make an
appointment with the principal, a school
counselor, and a mental health expert who is
experienced with bullying, and don't rule out
the possibility of changing schools.

NOT THAT

"It'll blow over."/"Who cares what he/she thinks?"/"Don't let it get to you so much."

—

If you research the long-term effects of bullying, you'll see that this is no small thing. Don't underestimate the impact of a bully.

When She's the Bully

Most parents of teenage daughters are prepared for run-ins with mean girls. When she contends with a little ugliness, it's unpleasant, but expected. Sooner or later, the wolves descend. But what do you do when the Big Bad Girl is your own daughter?

You don't expect to see the name that's lighting across your ringing cellphone. "Lynn" is the mother of your daughter's classmate, Katie. As your cell chirps urgently a second time, you rack your brains frantically, trying to remember how you ever even came to add Lynn as a contact and why.

Katie and your daughter have never particularly cared for one another. Anytime Katie's name came up in your household, your daughter would scoff then ask, "Katie *who*?"

By the third ring, you've come up empty but decide to pick up anyway. The voice on the other end of the line is overly polite and you feel awkward immediately.

"Hi, this is Lynn Carmichael calling."

"Lynn! How have you been? It's been a long time."

"Not great. Katie is very upset. She said your daughter has been taunting her at school. I've seen some pretty nasty comments from her on Katie's Instagram as well. I'm not sure if you knew, but I'm concerned and I wanted to bring it to your attention."

You open and close your mouth a few times, but no words come out. You're very glad that Lynn can't see your face.

Before you deal with your daughter, remember:

1. Electronics are a privilege, not a right. If she doesn't have anything nice to say, take away her podium.

2. Apologies are a good place to start, but that's about it.

3. Her moral compass is out of order. Make sure the next steps are guided by yours.

SAY THIS

"You will be apologizing sincerely and immediately. Mom/Dad and I will be the judge of your apology and your behavior. We'll be calling the school in the morning to let them know what's going on and we will be monitoring your every move. You're going to be joining us for a meeting with the school psychologist to determine the best way that you can repair the damage your behavior has inflicted on your classmate. Starting this week, you're also going to be volunteering every weekend to support children and teens who've experienced bullying. Your phone is gone until your mom/dad and I agree that you've rebuilt our trust."

—

It's time to get hyper-vigilant. Learn what goes on when you're not there and don't rely on her interpretation of events. Reach out to the school, a counselor, or other professionals for support.

Your daughter must correct every single thing she's done wrong—and then some. She's got a lot of changing to do, and for that, "sorry" is not nearly good enough.

NOT THAT

"Be nice. What you say and do really affects other people."

———

This problem won't go away; left unchecked, it will get bigger. If you don't take her bullying seriously, neither will she.

When You Want Her to Think Bigger

||||||||||||||||||||||||||||||||||||||||||||||||||||||||||||||||

By definition, teenagers occupy the middle ground between childhood and adulthood. Which end of the spectrum they lie closer to depends on a lot of things. While their brains try to work out the hormone situation, teens swing radically between impatient impulsivity and level-headed decisiveness. When her concerns are too small and her reactions are too big, how do you get her to start thinking like a grown up?

You start in on your nightly round of questioning, probing your family members for their perspectives on all that's happening in the world outside of you. Your daughter— lucky her—is first up. She's given her undivided attention to a pile of mashed potatoes, which she flies into her mouth so quickly you'd think she was inhaling them. As the heap begins to dwindle, she takes a nanosecond to breathe, finally allowing something other than potatoes into her mouth. You seize the opportunity to strike: "So, what do you think about the upcoming election?"

She jerks her head up, raises an eyebrow, looks around, then back at you. Pointing to her shoulder, she mouths the question: *Me?* When you nod, she takes another huge bite of mashed potatoes and a very long time to chew. Mouth closed, she shrugs and raises a pointer finger, as if she couldn't help it that she took a bite of food instead of answering your question. "Honestly . . . I don't care who wins."

"What do you mean? You don't have any opinion about it?"

"No. Why should I? It doesn't affect my life."

Horrified, you realize that *she absolutely believes this*.

Before you beg her to wake up and join the real world, remember:

1. Information is easier to swallow in small bites. You don't have to be a news junkie to keep up.

2. Caring about something is the start of everything. Talk about what matters to her, whether that's animal welfare, the arts, or just about anything else.

3. The more she feels entitled to an opinion, the more she'll want one.

SAY THIS

"Now that you're becoming a young adult, you have a responsibility to the world. Now is the time to shape your perspectives and really think about your place. I'm going to get a subscription to the the New York Times/Wall Street Journal/Time/Scientific American. *Let's pick one article a day to read and discuss."*

———

You're not selling the paper, you're selling young adulthood. And *that* she'll buy.

NOT THAT

"You have no clue what's going on in the world."/"You're too preoccupied with your own life."

———

You want the focus off of her, so talk about something else—like current events, for example. Then you can fill her in on everything she doesn't know.

When She Wants to Lose (a Healthy Amount of) Weight

Teenage girls can have a tricky relationship with weight. So as the parent of a teenage girl, you've probably encountered a wide range of advice for navigating that relationship; everything from "Don't talk about it!" to "Celebrate what her body can *do*, not what it looks like!" Like most extreme approaches, these aren't practical. So what *should* you do when she says those dirty words: "I want to lose some weight?"

Her hair is damp and matted against her forehead as she hops with concentration from her left foot to her right. Her arms swing in rhythm, keeping time to a song you can't hear. She turns her wrist to check the tracker resting on it and smiles at whatever news it brings her. In a burst of final energy, she pushes through a high-kneed run, holding her place, but moving viciously. As she rounds out the stationary sprint, the mission seems to come to a close, and she plucks a single headphone from her ear.

You turn your head quizzically to the side and she answers the question you didn't have to ask.

"I started a new workout routine. I want to lose a little bit of weight."

Before you launch a full-blown campaign to stop this project, remember:

1. Weight loss is not a one-way street to unhealthy habits and eating disorders.

2. If you treat weight change like it's a dangerous, slippery slope, from which nothing good can come, so will she.

3. You're not obligated to defend her looks because no one has actually attacked them.

SAY THIS

"If losing weight is an important goal for you, and you continue to have a healthy attitude and approach, then I am happy to support you. Let's go to the doctor to get a reference point of your height and weight and some on advice on how to go about this."

When it comes to figuring out what's healthy for your daughter, don't guess: Talk to your family doctor, a nutritionist, or a dietician for guidance, and let them outline checkpoints throughout the process. Here's an opportunity to teach a responsible approach to weight loss.

NOT THAT

"You don't need to lose any weight!"/"What are you talking about? You look great!"

———

Discourage every self-improvement and she'll start to doubt your honesty. If her goals are healthy and realistic, there's no reason not to keep them.

When She's Worried About a Big Change

As a parent, you probably want to make your daughter's life as easy and stress-free as you possibly can. The older she gets, the harder that becomes. Each stage of growing up brings changes bigger than the last and when the stakes are high, so are emotions—for better or worse. What do you do when the pressure is on and she's starting to crack?

Dread comes in many forms. Right now, it's jittery limbs and sweaty palms. Your daughter is fidgeting in her seat, shaking out her wrists. Every once in a while, she gives the squirmy dance a break to chew her nails to bits. You wonder how you can put an end to whatever's doing this.

"Sweetheart, how can I help?"

When she looks up at you, the tears welling in her eyes reach the brim and spill over. She wipes the tears away impatiently, almost angrily.

"I don't know! You can't. There's nothing you can do about it, I just have to deal with it. I wish there was something you could do, but you really can't. There's just so much going on and so much I have to take care of before the week is out and I don't know . . . *I'm freaking out!*"

Before you subscribe to that logic, remember:

1. If she tells you she's stressed out, you're lucky to be getting even that much information. Take it and *run*.

2. If you're tempted to tell her that she has nothing to worry about, consider how many times this bit of reassurance has helped you.

3. Anxiety works closely with insecurity. Take out one and you can start to take down the other.

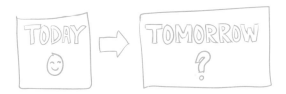

SAY THIS

"I'm sorry that you're stressed. The best way to fight nerves and anxiety is with knowledge and preparation. Let's make a list of which parts of this you're dreading most. Then, we'll practice the conversations, situations, and problems you think you'll run into. If anything comes up later, make a note of it—we can run through this as many times as you need."

—

Bring a flashlight into the woods and you'll find more trees than monsters.

NOT THAT

"It'll all work out!"/"Don't stress about it, you'll be fine!"

—

You may be right, but she doesn't feel prepared. And preparation is better served with action, not words.

When Everything Makes Her Anxious

When you were young, the word "worrywart" was probably thrown around a lot. Along with "Nervous Nellie" and "hand-wringer," it's a verbal pat on the back, a way to dismiss the perpetually worried. For most of us, anxiety is an unwelcome feeling that comes, then goes. But for some, worry doesn't leave quite as easily as that. You could blame a lack of trying, but you'd miss the mark. So, when anxiety tightens its grip on your daughter and won't let go, how do you free her from its grasp?

Even as a little girl, your daughter showed no shortage of carefulness. But that word no longer seems to apply. What was once quirky and maybe a little endearing looks different, now. She spreads the planner wide, then counts the handwritten items in her list, not once, not twice, but four separate times. She reads the tasks aloud, defensively, as if each is menacing.

"I have to: outline the history essay, meet with the math tutor, read the new biology chapter, practice the piano, organize my room, lay out my clothes for the morning, *and* do my laundry."

It's hard to understand where the fear in her voice stems from. You search the list for something remarkable and fail. It's all familiar and under her control, but you wouldn't know that by the sound of her voice.

"Sweetheart, it's *Saturday*. You've already done all of your homework. The math tutor's not coming for another hour. Why don't you give yourself a break?"

She glares at you, stupefied, as if you've just said something absolutely ridiculous. "Monday is going to be *terrible* if I don't start next week's stuff now. I *have* to do at least half of the list. At *least*."

As you wonder how on earth you're going to get her to chill out:

1. Imagine a world where feelings can be turned off like a light. Now wave goodbye. We don't live there.

2. Remember that anxiety is not a flaw in the design of personality. Don't treat it like one.

3. Be reasonable. If you're smart enough to know that you're not qualified to teach piano or tutor math, you're smart enough to know that you can't do the job of a mental health professional, either.

SAY THIS

"I've noticed that you rarely seem relaxed, even on the weekends."/"I know that you haven't been sleeping through the night."/"I hear how tense you sound, especially when you talk about what you have to do."

"I want you to have the most peaceful and happy life possible. I'm here to help you. Let's set up a chance for you to speak with someone about your anxiety."

—

Anytime your observations make *you* anxious, start recording. Use the Notes application on your phone, or write down what you notice. Keep track of the dates, times of day, and situations that seem to stress your daughter out.

When you seek professional help, hand over your data. It'll help them help her.

NOT THAT

"Just relax!"/"What are you always so worried about?"

———

Even if she can tell you what she's so worried about, she'll still worry about it. And if she could just relax, she'd have done it by now.

When the Sadness Isn't Lifting

|||||||||||||||||||||||||||||||||||||||||||||||||

Impatience, frustration, and angst may be the teenager's bread and butter, but not all bad moods are created equal. Sadness is a fact of life. But when sadness is the fact and life is an afterthought, adolescence is not the culprit. What do you do when she's been knocked down and isn't getting back up?

You hear the muted tones of the reality show she's been watching on a loop. You can't remember which caricature-like celebrity the public is meant to keep up with, but whoever it is, your daughter is doing her part. Sleep and TV are her most faithful companions now that she's all but abandoned her interests, which gather dust in recent memory. At first, you had no reason to question her claim that she was just feeling run down. But that was the first time that she spent a weekend in bed, with no flu to blame.

You interrupt the first binge-watch of the day, hoping against hope that you can convince her to do something—anything—else.

"What are you up to, Sweetheart?"

Her voice trails dully across the room and back to you. "Nothing. As usual."

"Don't you want to—"

"No."

"You didn't even hear what I had to say. You've got to be so bored in there. Stretch your legs. Go outside. You've got to get out of this room . . . "

"I said *no*."

As you fight to get back the happiness she's lost, remember:

1. Someone who is unmotivated won't take suggestions. Don't make change optional. It's time to call in an expert.

2. What she does is much more important than what she says. When it comes to feeling better, measure in actions, not words.

3. She will quit many times and this will tempt you to quit. Don't.

SAY THIS

"I've noticed that you don't seem to pursue art/music/writing like you used to."/"I haven't heard you laugh in a very long time."/"I've noticed that you seem to be taking more naps than usual."/"I've noticed that you seem tired and unmotivated."

"I love you and I'm concerned. I want to help. I think you'd really benefit from talking to someone outside the family, who can be totally objective with you. Let's find a counselor together. I want to help you pick someone who seems credible. Then we'll book an appointment."

———

When your daughter is not herself, don't ignore what you see. Trust your instincts.

Take every precaution, including and especially the help of a mental health professional.

NOT THAT

"Lighten up! You have nothing to be upset about."/"You're doing just fine."

—

If you sweep this under the rug, she may think twice before letting you see her sadness again.

When You Think
She's Hurting Herself

Self-harm is a practice you've probably heard of; one you hoped you'd never need to understand. Of all the things that can hurt your daughter, there's no pain like the kind that is self-inflicted. When she feels bad to feel better, how do you save her from herself?

It's a sweltering and still afternoon, the kind that is particular to early August days. You place yourself next to the air conditioner, hoping for a reprieve. You close your eyes and shiver blissfully as the cool air reaches your back. When you open them again, you see your daughter climbing down the stairs in a long t-shirt and jeans. She brushes past you without saying a word.

"Honey, aren't you *dying* in that shirt?"

Her return is immediate, almost rehearsed: "Nah. You know me, I'm always cold."

"There's no way you're comfortable in that."

She shrugs and flashes a smile, but you continue to peer at her until something on her wrist catches your eye. She shuffles her arms under her sleeves anxiously, then clasps her fingers to the edge and pulls them further down. But it's too late, you've seen it—the whitewashed jagged edge of a scar.

She needs you now more than ever. Be brave and remember:

1. Not everyone who self-injures is suicidal and not everyone who's suicidal self-injures. Don't assume either. Take every precaution.

2. Punishing someone who is punishing themselves is not likely to help.

3. Fighting pain with pain is her coping method. She needs help finding a new one.

SAY THIS

"I've made an appointment with the family doctor/psychiatrist/psychologist. I'm going to take you this afternoon."

—

Take her to an appointment with a mental health professional as soon as possible, no heads-up necessary.

NOT THAT

"I can't believe you're cutting!"/"Look at what you're doing to yourself!"/"No computer or phone until you stop."/"Why would you do that to yourself?"

——

Whatever your feelings, she needs professional support managing hers. Don't hesitate. Get help.

When Your Family Loses Someone You Love

||||||||||||||||||||||||||||||||||||||||||||||||||||||||||||||||||||||||||||||||||||

Grief is greedy and consuming. It arrives at your door uninvited and overstays a welcome it was never extended. When your family loses someone you love, every part of living is labor. The world lurches forward, despite everything, and the passage of time feels like an impossible betrayal. As you pull yourself through the aftermath, moment by moment, your daughter will try to do the same. How do you see her through the worst thing that could happen?

You share the heavy silence, gazing stony-eyed at the baseboard. The only sound is her drawn, haggard breathing. Every so often, a sob catches in her throat and she coughs until it's gone. She's slid her head onto your shoulder where it rests, motionless. The room is both very full and painfully empty.

You have forgotten how to think; speaking feels out of the question. But listening to your own thoughts is suffocating. Certain that you can't spend another second alone with them, you let out a weary, "I'm so sorry . . ."

She inhales sharply, holds her breath and begins to weep. You draw her in closer to you, wishing desperately for the comforting words you don't have.

Remember:

1. Shared grief isn't less painful, but it is lighter to carry.

2. Expression is the enemy of suffering, and it's not limited to talking.

3. Between ignoring and encouraging the ache of grief, there is a middle ground. Find it together.

SAY THIS

"Sweetheart, I share your heartache. Grief is one of worst kinds of pain we can ever experience. However you choose to express your pain, I am prepared to share, listen, hold you, or give you some space. When you're ready, we will talk about how to take the first steps back into your routines and the things you enjoy. Then let's research some support groups together."

———

You can't cut corners on the road to healing, but you don't have to go alone.

NOT THAT

"This is hard on me, too! I lost my dad/mom/ husband/wife!"

—

The way you express your pain will be the model for how she expresses her own.

Do the best you can to show her how to make it through loss.

When She Says the Teacher Hates Her

Your daughter's high school teachers may not be a permanent fixture in her life, but they get to decide whether she passes Go. The grades they assign and the recommendation letters they write (or don't) matter well beyond graduation day. So, when your daughter insists that plummeting grades are a sure sign the teacher hates her, should you plead her case?

She slams her folder onto the counter with a violent whack. In a one-armed, nonstop maneuver, she throws the top sleeve open and yanks the papers tucked inside. With a flick of her wrist they are tossed and spun evenly across the table top, landing squarely in front of you. You tilt your head at her, partly curious, mostly impressed, then look down at the document. It is her latest essay for English honors, returned with the grade, "C."

Both fists are pressed tightly against her hips. She taps her foot feverishly and watches you with more eye contact than anyone really needs. Her eyebrows are raised in indignation and don't fall back down. Sensing, perhaps, that you are not angry enough, she lifts an arm to point to the page in front of you and demands,

"Did you *see that*? Did you see? I can't believe it. *I can't believe it!* She gave me a 'C!' A 'C!' Do you know how many *hours* I spent on this paper? I did everything that she asked me to—literally, everything—and then some. What does she want from my life? She just hates me. There's no other explanation. *She hates me*."

Before you refute or support that claim, keep in mind:

1. It's not safe to assume that your daughter is right. Anger and accuracy don't have strong ties.

2. It's not safe to assume that her teacher is right, either. Adults can be wrong, too.

3. Disappointment in others comes much easier than disappointment in ourselves. This can make it tricky to spot the difference.

SAY THIS

"Well, let's talk about why you feel that way. What are some of the specific things he/she has said or done to make you think you're not liked? Let's focus on dealing with the individual problems and set up a meeting with your teacher."

—

When in school, do as the teachers do: ask her to support her argument—and cite it. Then go straight to the source and see the teacher.

NOT THAT

"Really?!/I'm going to talk to them!"/"Well, you're probably just slacking."

———

Don't take either side until you have all the information. Here's a chance to teach conflict resolution.

When She Steals from You

||||||||||||||||||||||||||||||||||||||||||||||||||||||||||||||||||||||||||||||||||||||||||||||||||||||||||||||||||||||||

Whether you're in the 1 percent or any part of the other 99, "I could really use a little less money," is probably not a thought that's ever entered your mind. When your savings start to dwindle, it's a bad feeling. When you don't know why, it's a worse feeling. What do you do when you discover that your very own flesh and blood is swindling your hard-earned funds?

As your dread mounts, you slash the envelope open with rough impatience. You wouldn't mind at all if the credit card statement it contained was ripped clean in half. You pluck the document bitterly, bracing yourself for the unpleasantness.

In a world where every bill is unwelcome and disappointing, this one takes the cake. The charges are so astronomical that they look ridiculous in writing. Your first instinct is to scold yourself—how on Earth did you let your spending get *THIS* bad? Then your senses return, and with them, logic. You *didn't* spend that much. You scour the charges for proof: beneath the routine grocery expenses, coffee indulgences, and birthday balloons from the 15th, you spot a very curious splurge, indeed. Bloomingdale's? Who, you wonder, spent $250 on Kate Spade?

You turn to your daughter, who stands up, tosses a crisp black leather purse over her shoulder and asks, "What?"

"... *nice bag you've got there.*"

Before you throw that overpriced totem of total betrayal into the fireplace, remember:

1. Even if she watches it burn, she won't learn what it means to burn money. And that is an important lesson.

2. She didn't buy that bag—you did. It's about time you were reimbursed.

3. She broke your wallet and you trust. Both need fixing.

SAY THIS

"You've stolen not just something of ours, but our trust in you. You'll have to earn that—and the money—back. We're going to take 10 percent of your work paychecks per week until we make up the money you stole, to give you a sense of the loss./We're going to outline chores and assign dollar values to them—you'll earn the money back through the work you put in."

—

Show her the high cost of a cheap thrill. If this becomes a repeat problem, seek professional support.

NOT THAT

"YOU COULD GO TO JAIL FOR THIS!"

—

Show, don't tell. Bring your daughter to meet with your town's police precinct, or the security team in a department store, supermarket, or pharmacy. Let *them* talk to her about what happens to teenagers who commit petty crimes.

When She Needs to Pick a University

||||||||||||||||||||||||||||||||||||||||||||||||||||||||||||||||||||||||||

Decision-making, especially on a large scale, can feel like risky business. Throw in stakes that include everything from the next four years of life to future job placement you're well on your way to Stress City. For your daughter, choosing her university is a euphemism for choosing her destiny. And while it's not so simple as that, it's a heavy burden, nonetheless. How can you help her lighten the load?

Some responses have returned, other have not. The deadlines approach, just the same. She stares blankly at the latest letter to have made its way to the mailbox. Whatever gears were turning in her brain seem to have gotten stuck. Cautiously, you ask what the letter says.

"I got in," she replies, a little breathless.

"Well, what's wrong? That's *great* news!"

"I guess . . ." her voice trails off. Her gaze stays fixed on the letter, her brow furrowed with intense concentration. She stays there for a moment, lost in her own head. "It's just . . ."

"What is it?"

She looks up at you helplessly. "I applied to so many schools. Some of my top choices didn't take me. Other ones did, but they're far away. Then there's the state schools I got into. They're less expensive than my top choices, but I don't know if I'll like them as much. And so far, I only got into one of the same schools as my friends. We were supposed to go together. How am I supposed to choose where I want to go?"

When it's time to help her make the biggest decision of her life (so far), remember:

1. Stress is exhausting and contagious, but preparation is a cure-all.

2. Big decisions are made from a lot of little decisions. Start small.

3. If the options weren't great and many, choosing wouldn't be this hard. What she's got is too much of a good thing.

SAY THIS

"Here's what we're going to do; we're going to visit the schools you're interested in. For the schools we can't visit, we're going to take a virtual tour. We're going to look at the curricula, departments, size, classroom ratios, etc. Then we're going to send emails to the professors at the schools you're interested in. I'll be your parent-partner in picking a university."

———

By the time she's done, she'll really be ready for college.

NOT THAT

"Well, it all depends on where you get in."

—

It depends on a lot of other things, too. Explore all the possibilities before you start to rule them out.

When She Wants to Transfer to Another High School

As the parent of a teenage daughter, you've probably heard the declaration "I *hate* school" enough times for it to have lost its impact. It's a phrase that can mean anything from "I don't want to do my homework" to "It's early on a Monday morning." But even if you always considered it wishful thinking to hope that school leaves your daughter satisfied and smiling, the words "I want to transfer" bring things to a new level. What do you do when she not only "hates" school but hates it so much that she wants a new one?

It is Sunday night, and familiar weekday dread has nestled in comfortably, though you wouldn't know it by looking around the restaurant, which is brimming and buzzing with loud families not unlike your own. It is the same local favorite you frequent every Sunday night. The whole bunch of you are huddled into your tried-and-tested corner booth, gobbling the last surviving appetizers.

As far as the Sunday Blues go, your daughter seems to have been hit hardest, and harder than usual, at that. She's leaning her head against the barrier separating your table from the next; a small patch of hair slides up as her head sinks slowly down. It's not until her head is sideways against her shoulder that she bothers to pick it up. Her mozzarella sticks have long since gone cold.

She takes a tiny bite, then wipes her face. After setting the napkin down cautiously, she clasps her hands together and rests them on the table in front of her. She eyes you very seriously and you know what's going on—she's about to make a case. But for what or why, you don't know.

"Guys, before you say no, I want you to just think about what I'm saying. This school is really not working out for me. I have zero friends there. I'm bored every single weekend. I don't like any of the clubs and I haven't made a single team. I've been thinking about it a lot and I just think I'd be so much happier if I transferred to another school. I am so sick of Fairview High."

Whether you're about to say "Tough luck, you're staying" or "OK, let's get you out of there" or something in between, first, remember:

1. A new school could mean new problems. Or old problems. Or no problems. There's a lot to consider here.

2. There are a lot of reasons why your daughter may want to transfer schools; what they are matters, and they matter a lot.

3. Whether she goes or stays, there will be problems to fix.

SAY THIS

"Let's figure out the reasons you're feeling this way. If we feel that the reasons are serious enough, we'll go look at a different high school and see if you can spend a day shadowing there. If not, I'd like you to give it one full semester/ quarter/marking period. We're going to try to invite a couple of different girls over; we're going to try a couple of different school clubs. Let's check in once a week to see how things are going; if not, every night, I'm here for you, whatever you need."

—

You can't treat the problem until you identify it.

NOT THAT

"Give it time."/"You're doing fine!"

—

You may mean to help or teach perspective when you minimize the problem.

But when you tell your daughter how to feel, she may not come to you the next time she's got a problem. Before you draw any conclusions, listen carefully.

SECTION 58

When You Think She Might Be Doing Drugs

||||||||||||||||||||||||||||||||||||||||||||||||||||||||||||||||||||||||||||||||||||||||||||||||||||||

Drugs are the loathsome and fearsome enemy of all those who love a teenager. So, what do you do when the enemy is at the gates, ready to invade?

Your daughter is not home yet. This fact, on its own, sounds simple and uneventful. But the fact of the matter is that she's missed the curfew so radically that *late* is no longer the right word to describe her—she's *absent*. She'd promised to leave the party by 1 a.m. When that didn't happen, you were annoyed. When your phone calls, text messages, and voicemails went unanswered, you felt concern creep in. When one hour turned to two, concern exploded into complete and total anxiety. Since then, you've stalked around the kitchen like a ghost; wide-eyed and wired with panic.

When she clods back in through the door, you learn that it is possible to feel absolute rage and total relief at the exact same moment. Her eyes are heavily laden, slightly red. *Has she been crying?* She cracks a slow, cartoonish smile and you rule this possibility out immediately. "Heeeeey," she coos. The rage starts to eclipse your relief.

And perhaps you are not in the best position to think rationally, but think and think you do. Suddenly, the weird things you've noticed over the past few weeks no longer seem meaningless or unrelated. You think of the way she clambered awkwardly to the bathroom last weekend, insisting that her stomach hurt. You think of how wildly her mood swings have outdone themselves, both in the way of intensity and number. Before you can stop it, the idea enters your brain: *She's taking drugs.*

Before you launch this investigation, remember:

1. You should ask her if she's taking drugs—but only if the truth does not interest you.

2. You don't have to guess, because drug tests exist.

3. If she's not taking drugs, she's got nothing to lose from proving it.

SAY THIS

"I'd like you to take a drug test. The results will give us the truth, no matter what the outcome. It gives you a chance to prove yourself and gives me the assurance that you are safe."

—

Don't get into an argument about trust, there's no argument to be had. Now is the time for truth.

Anytime you suspect your daughter may be using drugs, get her an appointment with a health care professional immediately. If you have to fib to get her to there, so be it.

NOT THAT

"Are you taking drugs?!"/"I know you're taking drugs!"

———

You're not likely to get any useful information from questions and you definitely won't get any from accusations.

When You're Very Sick

|||||||||||||||||||||||||||||||||||||||||||||||||||||||||||||||||||||||||||||||||||||||||||||||||||||||||||||||||

As the parent of a teenage daughter—and, actually, as any human being at all—you're probably aware by now that life doesn't always go the way we'd hoped. Getting the news that you are seriously ill can be crippling and devastating. When the burden you're carrying is so heavy, how do you keep shouldering the weight of family?

The exhausting, torturing wait is over. In the place of charts, scans, and vague assurances from doctors that they don't really know what it is yet comes the diagnosis. Paralysis is not meant to be a symptom, but it strikes you, anyway. You sit motionlessly and quietly in the sterile, white room for a long time.

When you return home, you no longer feel paralyzed. You are not glued to time and space. Instead, you hover somewhere between your body and mind, feeling as though neither belongs to you. Your daughter races to meet you, eager for each and every new piece of information. She is impatient and worried, but you aren't speaking. You are searching frantically and desperately for words. Words of comfort you can give her, words that spare her, words that reveal a different and better truth.

Remember:

1. The more painful it is to talk about it, the more important it is to talk about it.

2. Information is power, even if you can't change it.

3. Families are not made of fair-weather friends. You are loved no matter what.

SAY THIS

"Please know that we are going to keep you informed about my health each step of the way. As hard as this is, we will support each other through the changes we're undergoing. Let's have a family meeting to talk about how daily life will shift and to figure out what we can do to help carry each other's burdens. We have to be extraordinarily open with each other. Don't try to shield me from your feelings. You're my child and I love you; I have to know when you're feeling hurt."

—

Love doesn't care about your conditions.

NOT THAT

Nothing.

—

She needs your words. She needs you.

When You Were Wrong

||||||||||||||||||||||||||||||||||||||||||||||||||||||||||||||||||||||||||||||||||||||||||||||||||||

There may come a time—in a faraway place and in the distant future—when pigs can fly and when you, somehow, are *wrong*. When and if this sad, bizarre day arrives, you may feel completely unprepared. After all, this will have *never, ever* happened before. So, what on earth do you do?

Your words hang in midair as the realization sinks in. You take a sharp and sudden breath, scrambling to take them back, but it's too late. You already released them; they're gone. Your daughters' eyes widen and flash toward you. They are glinting with a level of satisfaction that borders on pure joy. Her cheeks wrinkle up, like drapes drawn apart to let in sunlight, and she beams. You may not be prepared, but she, on the other hand, has been waiting for this moment for a very, very long time. A frenzy has begun.

You slip directly into defense mode, preparing at hyper-speed for the things she will throw at you, scrambling for loopholes that prove that you are, in fact, correct. But it is all in vain. No matter which way you look at it, you are totally and completely wrong.

Before you melt into a puddle of shame and sorrow, remember:

1. The way *you* act when you're wrong becomes the way *she* acts when she's wrong.

2. Being wrong is only as bad as you make it seem.

3. Your daughter got it right. Don't you hope that happens a lot in her life?

SAY THIS

"I want to let you know that you were right earlier. I made a mistake. I'm sorry and I'm glad you spoke up."

—

There's no burn if you pass the torch.

NOT THAT

"Don't contradict me."

—

Do let her contradict you. Be willing to apologize. There's dignity in humility.

INDEX

A

accidents, 140–43
actions, 237
addiction, 174
advice, 48–51, 58–59
advocates, 50
alcohol, 172–75
answers, 43, 63, 128
anxiety, 196–99
applications, 12–15
argument, 214
assumptions, xiii, 114, 205, 213
attention, 117
audience, 54

B

best friends, 36–39
betrayal, 37
boredom, 92–95
boyfriends, 20–23, 68–71
bribes, 47
bullies, 176–83

C

change, 89, 192–95
choices, 170
chores, 8–11
classmates, 180
cleanliness, 112–15
clothing, 24–27, 72–75
community, 90, 162
comparisons, 136

confidence, 82
conflict, 134, 215
confrontation, 173
connection, 106
control, 91, 111
conversation, 62
cooperation, 45

D

decisions, 145, 220–23
defeat, 101
definitions, 113
disappointment, 144, 213
distress, 1
divorce, 152–55
drugs, 228–31

E

eating disorder, 148–51, 189
effects, 179
embarrassment, 80–83
entitlement, 103
Europe, 41
example, 166
experience, x, 97, 122
expression, 209, 211

F

family, 153–54
fear, 197
fight or flight, 53
focus, 102
free will, 44

G

goals, 13, 146, 191
grades, 212
gratitude, 96–99
grief, 208–11
guilt, 30

H

hair, 64–67
hate, 116–19
healing, 123, 125, 210
heartbreak, 124–27
help, 85, 98
Huddy, Jessica Yuppa, xi
humility, 239
hurt, 86, 121

I

ideas, 26
illness, 232–35
inclusion, 105
information, 185, 233
instructions, xii–xiii, 115
interests, 94
Internet, 5
intimacy, 70

J

jealousy, 132–39

K

knowledge, 73
Kukoff, Ilana, xi

L

language, 118
likability, 120–23
listening, 33, 177, 227
looks, 32–35
love, 157, 234
lying, 28–31

M

memory, 163
mental health, 202, 206
mistakes, 238
moments, 158, 162–63
moods, 52–55
morality, 181
moving, 88–91

N

negotiation, 44, 129, 130

O

observations, 198
organization, 114

P

parents, 96, 110, 153, 222
passive aggression, 133
peers, 81
permission, 108–11
perseverance, 126
perspective, 184
phone, 164–67
planning, 14, 42

popularity, 104–7
power, 109
preparation, 194, 221
presentation, 74
pride, 135
problems, 65, 87, 110,
    218, 225
prom, 84

R

rationale, 131
reading, 18
reasons, 29, 226
rejection, 100–103
relationships, 22
responsibility, 10, 99, 190
right, 56
rules, xii–xiii, 129

S

sadness, 200–203
self-esteem, 138
self-harm, 204–7
selfies, 25, 34
self-respect, 21
sexting, 168–71
sexuality, 156–59
shame, 169
sharing, 6–7
silence, 17
skills, 38
social media, 4–7
stealing, 216–19

stress, xiv–3, 193
suicide, 205
support, 178, 182

T

talking, 16–19
tantrums, 77
teachers, 212–15
texting, 165
threats, 46
time, 8–11
tone, 78, 162
transfers, 224–27
transgender, 160–63
travel, 40–43
trust, 217
truth, 229–30

U

understanding, 60–63, 130

V

voice, 76–79

W

weight loss, 186–91
words, ix
worry, 3, 149, 192–95
wrong, 57, 236–39

Andrews McMeel Publishing
a division of Andrews McMeel Universal
1130 Walnut Street, Kansas City, Missouri 64106

www.andrewsmcmeel.com

18 19 20 21 22 SHO 10 9 8 7 6 5 4 3 2 1

ISBN: 978-1-4494-8805-5

Library of Congress Control Number: 2017940434

Editor: Patty Rice
Art Director/Designer: Julie Barnes
Illustrator: Hannah Luechtefeld
Production Editor: David Shaw
Production Manager: Carol Coe

ATTENTION: SCHOOLS AND BUSINESSES
Andrews McMeel books are available at quantity discounts with
bulk purchase for educational, business, or sales promotional use.
For information, please e-mail the Andrews McMeel Publishing
Special Sales Department: specialsales@amuniversal.com.